Calling a Halt to Mindless Change

A Plea for Commonsense Management

John Macdonald

AMACOM

American Management Association International

New York • Atlanta • Boston • Chicago • Kansas City • San Francisco • Washington, D.C.
Brussels • Mexico City • Tokyo • Toronto

This publication is designed to provide accurate and authoritative
information in regard to the subject matter covered. It is sold with
the understanding that the publisher is not engaged in rendering
legal, accounting, or other professional service. If legal advice or
other expert assistance is required, the services of a competent
professional person should be sought.

Library of Congress Cataloging-in-Publication Data

Macdonald, John, 1929–
    Calling a halt to mindless change : a plea for commonsense
management / John Macdonald.
        p.   cm.
    Includes bibliographical references and index.
    ISBN 0-8144-0349-2
    1. Organizational change.   I. Title.
HD58.8.M217   1997
658.4'02—dc21   97-48808
                                                         CIP

Printing number

10   9   8   7   6   5   4   3   2   1

In an era of change
this book is optimistically dedicated
to a future that
our grandchildren will inherit

for
Andrew, Natalie, Lucas, Daniel,
Gareth, Adam, and James

Contents

Preface

Originally to be entitled *Between Gods,* this book set out to describe a world beset with change: a world in which whole nations, let alone businesses, were cast adrift in a leaky boat, on an ocean in turmoil, and without a compass. My arrogant intention was to provide a compass for future management; but in reality it was just another change management book.

However, my research began to challenge the original concept. I kept finding companies that seemed to be sailing through all the storms of change. As I examined the management practices and long-term success of 3M, Arthur Andersen, Marks and Spencer, Wal-Mart, J. Sainsbury, Toyota, Procter and Gamble, Motorola, and others, I found a new perspective. These companies were continuously successful over long periods but didn't need reengineering or any of the other popular "revolutionary" changes. They appeared to anticipate external change long before their competitors. They met serious problems and made mistakes. It was not all smooth sailing, but their fundamental seamanship (that is, their value systems) meant that they were rarely faced with the need for radical reorganization.

I revisited my own experience in corporate life and began to realize that the business world's clamor for change and fads was nothing new. Present throughout the century, it exploded in the postwar years of the 1950s and has been accelerating ever since.

For many companies, each new fad or phase of change or vaunted wisdom has left another layer of accepted barnacles that in time encrust the organization and impede progress. For others, with their own strong value systems, the new "ism" is absorbed, rejected, or adapted to strengthen the existing culture.

The result is that this book turned out rather differently from how I began it. It now aims to examine both sides of the coin.

The degree of change currently being advocated by a host of change masters is not only nonsense but is positively wicked advice for the majority of organizations. They are not capable of implementing the reengineering proposed without devastating impact on the company and the people who work within it. Downsizing is a child of this process. The companies that really do need radical reengineering are the victims of a previous and long period of mindless management. Executives should listen to the siren song of change with a healthy dose of scepticism. A return to common sense is long overdue.

Some of the changes highlighted by the consulting gurus are desirable. But in practical business terms, they are better envisaged as *evolutionary* rather than revolutionary changes. The central section of this book emphasizes the point that the *real* pace of change is well within the normal decision-making cycles of executives. All of the envisioned changes could have been or can be anticipated and thus planned for. There is no need to panic or to fear change, if anticipated change can provide a host of positive advantages.

This book now argues for a new breed of managers who reject the helter skelter of mindless change initiated by mindless management. Instead, the book encourages managers to view the future in terms of evolutionary common sense.

Acknowledgments

This book was not created by a lone author in a closed room. Writing is a culmination of shared experiences, relationships, and thoughts with many people over a long time. This motley band of friends, clients, and colleagues (these are not mutually exclusive categories) provide continual stimuli and constructive criticism. I view them all as collaborators. Even if some are not mentioned, they are not forgotten.

The direction of this particular book changed over a relatively short period of time. Life's infirmities also provided their interruptions. These published acknowledgments are therefore confined to the band of people who stayed on hand to help me through the change and the delays.

Linda Rae Baldwin, who jumps out of airplanes but otherwise has her feet on the ground.

Jean Biggs, who has shared her own business traumas and success.

Cheryl Brodie, who has the incisive intelligence to puncture balloons but somehow always leaves me encouraged.

J. K. and Shali Chandna, special friends who provide eternal values for a changing society.

Sarah Dawson, with whom I share a birthdate (though she insists that the year was different) and have achieved much together.

Professor Barry Davies, of Manchester University of Science and Technology, the quiet guru of British research and thought into management practices.

Helen and George Farmer and Marian Paradis, whose conversation on long summer evenings in Provence added wit to the wine.

Linda Fox of La Jolla, California, president of Objectives International, a feisty lady who makes little room for compromise.

Professor Al Gini, of Loyola University Chicago, a great motivator and a leader in the growing field of business ethics.

Adrienne Hickey, a patient editor who manages to combine warm flattery with a no-nonsense clarity of objective.

Brian Long, in all my business life the manager I most admire.

Ian Matthews, though it goes against the grain to include my accountant; however, he shared so much in the early incubation of an idea that he must share the blame for the result.

Joe McNally, with whom more than twenty-five years of business association and friendship have created a bond of trust I value beyond compare.

Dr. Madhav Mehra, a master at bringing people and ideas together.

Stephen Potts, who manfully carries the burden of being the author's son-in-law; his own career with one of the companies I highlight provided many insights for this book.

Faith Ralston, who has been an inspiration to me since we first started our collaboration in the late 1970s and with whom I have learned to share so much; her recent and powerful book *Hidden Dynamics* brings her long-overdue recognition.

Jenny Riley, a tireless politician who remembers me as I was and won't stand any nonsense; she confirms that a truthful friend is a great gift.

Sheila Stevenson, long-term friend and collaborator (I have forgiven her change of nationality from English to American—just !), who organized so much of my research that I sometimes think she should have done the writing.

Steve Tanner, a collaborator in several previous books who always has strong practical answers to philosophical questions.

Pat Tyre, who was working in Thailand for much of the gestation period of this book; our constant faxes and long telephone calls helped me wrestle with new concepts.

There are others who contributed and supported. But I cannot close without expressing my thanks to the contribution of my family. Sarah, my daughter, and Sharon, my daughter-in-law, have provided wonderful secretarial support. Stephen and Nicholas, my sons, are successful businessmen in their own right; together with daughter-in-law Liz, who is taking a business degree, they have continuously acted as informative sounding boards. Together with my wife, Anne, they make it all worthwhile.

Finally, I acknowledge Crystal Palace Football Club and Surrey County Cricket Club, which like life itself provide many frustrations combined with moments of sheer ecstasy.

Part One

Mindless Change

These opening chapters examine the multiplicity of -isms and false gods that have confused management and obscured the simple truths of business.

Chapter 1

Between Gods

Change and decay in all around I see
O thou, who changest not, abide with me.
> Hymn "Abide with Me." H. F. Lyte (1840)

All we have gained by our unbelief
Is a life of doubt diversified by faith,
For one of faith diversified by doubt:
We called the chessboard white—now we call it black.
> Elizabeth Barrett Browning (1806–1861)

The last decade has been characterized by a mounting clamor for change. The siren voices of revolution seem to permeate every aspect of life. In religion, politics, society, and business, the past is derided. The future is declared to be uncertain and unpredictable. A high priesthood of gurus and change masters offer tempting panaceas for managing the revolution of change. At their behest, many managers are abandoning old verities, methods, and values. They are caught between gods. The change masters are causing havoc. It is time to call a *halt* to this *mindless change*. At the least, we should pause for thought.

This book is about business. The world of business does not exist or operate in a vacuum. It has to comprehend and adapt to the changing circumstances in which it operates. So business is always about change. Organizations that do not recognize that change is a continuous process in need of managing are condemned to periodic uncontrolled revolutions. They become susceptible to legions of consultants ever eager to propose ready-

3

made solutions. In the context of individual companies and even business as a whole, most of these radical changes are not only mindless; they are positively dangerous.

The need for radical change in the way business is organized and managed is exaggerated. Above all, the nature of how change is being implemented is causing a lot of damage to companies, and to the men and women who work in them. Downsizing is only one example of knee-jerk reactions to this clamor for change.

This book argues that:

- Executives are losing sight of the simple truths of business.
- Many organizations are throwing the baby out with the bathwater.
- A healthy dose of common sense is long overdue.
- The secret of business success is nurtured evolution rather than revolution.

The conventional wisdom of the change masters tends to concentrate on examples such as Xerox, IBM, and Texas Instruments. Almost every major conference on business process reengineering or other change management subject includes a speaker from one of these companies. Their presentations explain how their great corporations recognized the need to change; they revel in telling how they went about it. But these are very misleading case histories. The real lesson to be learned from these and other examples is not the traditional scenario of Phoenix rising from the ashes. Rather, what caused the original fire? In truth, as we see later, these case histories are more pertinent as evidence of earlier, catastrophic failure of their management to understand the evolutionary nature of their respective markets. IBM compounded the issue by losing touch with its value systems or fundamental culture. More than sixty thousand loyal and company-proud employees lost their jobs, and in many cases their self-esteem.

Evolution, Not Revolution

Most businesses need evolution, not revolution. The scope and reverberations of radical change are extremely hard to control.

As a consequence, the results are rarely as envisaged. Throw a pebble, even a long sequence of pebbles, into a pool and the ripples quietly touch and influence every corner of the pool. Throw in a large rock, and the results are usually chaotic. The water is displaced, the banks are damaged, and the fish are stunned or killed. The ecology of the pool will take time to re-cover. When considering change, executives must avoid the temptation to hurl rocks. Instead, they must encourage their em-ployees to practice a pattern of continuous pebble throwing, such that the requisite mass of change is absorbed with minimal disruption of what is healthy in the company.

In the 1980s, many corporations became so obsessed with *quality* and/or their current rating on Wall Street that they lost focus on the essential processes and patterns of their business. Many failed to anticipate the changing shape of markets and, per-haps more important, the coming convergence of familiar and mature technologies. They didn't recognize the need, let alone take the evolutionary steps that were necessary, to maintain their competitive advantage. Systemic lack of comprehension of what was happening during this period was exemplified by the low investment in development and training of employees to meet the future. Yet during the same period, the evolutionary compa-nies (of which more later) were driving technology suppliers to adapt their products to meet their perceived needs. It is not an accident that the evolutionary companies were also substantially increasing their investment in educating and training their em-ployees.

In the 1990s, complacent companies were desperately try-ing to play catch-up. Among them were great names renowned for their excellent management, such as IBM and Eastman Kodak. But no problem: Hammer and Harvard were on hand to help them.

Michael Hammer wrote *Reengineering the Corporation*, which captured the minds of some business leaders. Of even more relevance to my thesis is that his book was subtitled "A Manifesto for Business Revolution." The dust jacket copy went on to exclaim, "Forget what you know about how business should work—most of it is wrong."

Harvard University wanted to encourage new thinking and so provided strong support to the revolution through yet more case histories (see Chapter 5). Corporate executives got the message that they were now free to indulge in an orgy of rock hurling. Their stagnant pools were soon in turmoil and their desperate employees were left either searching for life belts or drowned.

In retrospect, it is now clear that the major mistake of many executives was not that they engaged in business process reengineering and downsizing but that they so mindlessly and irresponsibly implemented these concepts. Hammer now accepts that the concepts went too far in implementation, but a gentle slap on the wrist for naïvete does not absolve many so-called business leaders of blatant irresponsibility.

A root cause of this period of disorder is that senior management, faced with external pressures, spent its time arguing the concepts with their gurus or, more likely, the senior partners of their favorite consulting companies. They then made decisions with little reference to their own organizations' real culture or the problems of those tasked with implementation. It was delegated to middle managers or specialists who were expected to work closely with the consultant organization's delegated implementers. In no time, the blind were leading the blind.

The consulting companies, great and small, must take their share of the responsibility for mindless change. The market opportunity for the change masters grew rapidly as the reengineering fad gained credence. They needed to recruit to handle the available business. So they trawled the universities and business colleges, and soon thousands of new graduates and M.B.A.s were *helping* these great corporations reengineer their operations. Bemused middle management was caught between a rock and a hard place. Executive command culture and "whiz-kid" presentations of new process charts promising radical improvement in all facets of their business bemused everyone. Their "outside the box" answers to operational issues were in reality mere sound-bite understanding of the new concepts.

Looking over their shoulders at Wall Street, executives wanted to show dramatic improvement. They considered that they were facing a crisis to the extent that crisis management was necessary. From then on, cold-blooded (realistic!) business flow and system charts were the arbiters in deciding the careers of dedicated people. Now, a few years later, companies are beginning to understand the price of their decisions. They had sacrificed many of their best people. We are now witnessing reemployment of those who are considered to have significant skills. Or in other cases, the same people are being retained as consultants or playing a part in "outsourcing."

One expensive lesson of the early 1990s is that the degree of radical change called for and often implemented was in reality disastrous to the long-term interest of the organizations involved. James Belasco wrote a book in the 1980s in which he wanted the corporate elephants to learn to dance. There is considerable common sense in the book, but the net result is that our society has since endured herds of dancing elephants crushing the culture and value systems of good companies.

Business can learn, however, from the substantial number of great companies that have sailed serenely through all the storms of change. They continue to grow, succeed, and encompass the change around them without sacrificing their fundamental values; one should say it is *because* of those values. From the outset, these visionary companies have created organizations that naturally anticipate and manage change. They do not get involved in revolution or reengineering. They educate and empower their people long before these concepts become part of management jargon. They practiced prevention and managed quality decades before quality guru Philip Crosby wrote *Quality Is Free*. They were never part of the menagerie of dancing elephants and four-legged absolutes. They understood that, paradoxically, change almost always takes you back to where you once were.

Later in this chapter, we take up exploration of the management practices of a number of evolutionary companies. In the meantime, as an interesting aside to the arguments of this chapter, I ask the reader a question. Can you call to mind any anecdote or news item about the companies listed below in which there was any element of downsizing, reengineering, or fundamental repositioning of their market stance?

United States

- Procter and Gamble
- 3M

International

- Toyota
- Marks and Spencer

United States
- Arthur Andersen
- Wal-Mart
- Hewlett-Packard

International
- Canon
- J. Sainsbury
- Sony

All of these companies retained a close customer focus and therefore an understanding of customer needs, often before the needs were recognized by the customers themselves. They also developed their people to recognize in advance the possible impacts of new technologies and new management practices.

Revolutionary Hype

In reality, most of the revolutionary changes said to threaten modern enterprises are nothing of the sort. They are relatively slow-moving evolutions that are taking place well within the perspective of intelligent executives and their decision-making cycles. The pace of change only appears to be fast when we use false analogies with the time measures of past ages. People have always adapted to change (and often amazingly quickly; watch children with computers) and have at their command technologies that make those archaic time measures irrelevant.

An outstanding characteristic of the leading managers of evolutionary companies is that they always seem to have time to make a decision. They never confuse decision making with status symbols or some perceived need for macho-management. The increasing role of women at the highest level of management may well be one evolutionary change that will support this move to management maturity. A new manager is emerging who is not to be stamped upon by the circus masters of change and instant reaction.

The apostles of revolutionary change cite the technological revolution and the collapse of the communist "evil empire" as examples to demonstrate their thesis. The theory is that we are living in a period of tumultuous change. Even a cursory examination of each of these so-called revolutions serves to make the point that both were in reality slow-moving evolutions. Both were relatively obvious to those who had eyes to see and ears to listen. They were certainly predicted by well-publicized commentators at least three decades before they made a major impact on business. (We examine both "revolutions" in Chapters 7 and 8.) The interesting point is that there is evidence that most of the evolutionary firms anticipated the main elements of social and technological evolution long before their competitors did.

Technology Changes Slowly

The really remarkable fact about technology is not the speed but the *slowness* of change it brings about in business. Historically, this is common to the introduction of all technological advance. There is a delay between the promulgated and proven concept and the ready availability of cost-effective, easy-to-use applications of new techniques. An element in the delay is the time it takes potential users to comprehend fully what is available. Today we are discussing information technology (IT), but the same pattern can be discerned in the introduction of steam, the internal combustion engine, the telephone, radio, television, and the airplane.

Information technology has followed the traditional path. Just as early automobiles and railroad carriages were designed to look like stagecoaches, so early computers were used to duplicate hand-written processes. This is particularly true of business applications and systems developed by those with technology expertise rather than business experience. Hopefully, Microsoft may well be evidence of the convergence of these streams of knowledge. They have provided us all with the ability to take ownership of technology for our own ends. Certainly information technology now provides the entrepreneur with greater opportunities to open the future for all of us.

Little Has Really Changed

The *Harvard Business Review* celebrated its seventieth anniversary in November 1992 by inviting some of its long-term contributors to comment on their earlier statements. Almost without exception, their comments echo a central theme of this book: change is a slow process. Peter Drucker discussed an article he had written in 1961 entitled "This Competitive World." His view was that few had listened and that the "most noteworthy feature is that the article could have been written yesterday." Again, a fundamental contributor to management theory, Frederick Herzberg, commented, "One more time, what have I been saying since the 1950s."

Though Peter Drucker noted that little had changed over the years, he was an apparent enthusiast for the process reengineering revolution from its outset. His name was used strongly in the marketing of Michael Hammer and James Champy's book *Reengineering the Corporation.* He is quoted as saying "Reengineering is new, and it has to be done." No doubt he would have been horrified at the extremes of downsizing that reengineering spawned, but it does indicate that even wise old owls are tempted by revolution.

Chateau Generals

If change is relatively easy to predict, why do so many organizations fail to anticipate it? Why do so many seem unable to escape their past or to envisage their future?

In essence, they lose touch with the world outside. Many executives act like the generals of World War I. They and their staff sit in corporate headquarters or chateaux way behind the real front line. In 1916 Generals Haig and Gough of the British Army in France constantly pressed for futile and costly attacks on the Somme, when soldiers could barely drag one foot after another out of the sucking mud. Haig's chief of intelligence, Brigadier Gen. Charteris, who presumably should have warned him of the conditions at the front, was himself based in the headquarters chateau. Nearly two months after the battle had started, Charteris decided to visit the battlefield. While still a mile away, he commented to the local commander that he hadn't realized how bad the conditions were. His companion laconically replied, "It's worse up front, sir."

Too many executives act like chateau generals. The leadership of companies loses contact with the reality of the marketplace and with its own business. As a result, leaders are blinded by current performance and do not feel the need to be challenged by the future. When change eventually catches up with them, they react in panic. This may take the guise of vicious downsizing or other forms of beating up on the workers—the poor soldiers of our analogy.

The recent history of IBM is a perfect example of this corporate pattern. A decade ago, IBM was being extolled as the leader in all that was best in modern management. We were led to believe that the success of the corporation was based on empowerment of a workforce that was encouraged, by plaques in every office, to think. This thinking workforce was one of the few in the Western world that seemed to have a job for life. But these thinkers were blinded by current performance. Their factories produced the most advanced large computers in the world. They provided world-class support and service for these large computers. They were also considered world leaders in the field of total quality management. The only snag was that the marketplace, their customers, had decided that now they wanted small computers rather than large ones, however good the latter might be. Within a short period, sleek new sharks such as Compaq, Hewlett-Packard, and Apple with its Macintosh were ripping apart the great whale IBM. In the great chateaux of the World Trade Center, Poughkeepsie, and Armonk, the IBM generals panicked and sixty thousand thinkers were gone. The ironic footnote was that deep in the cellars of the IBM chateau the thinkers had developed the best-quality small computer ideally suited to the new market conditions. The initial market power of the IBM PC was dissipated by leaders blinded by the revenue performance of *rented* large machines. In fairness to IBM, it may yet become a positive example among the evolutionary companies. Its value systems are so strong that it gives evidence of surviving this catastrophe and returning to the forefront.

Changing Perceptions

Since the middle of the last century, scientific and technical advances have enhanced the ability of diverse civilizations and cultures to communicate and expand shared knowledge. The converging development of railroads, steamships, automobiles, and the airplane have provided global mobility. People now regularly move outside their familiar and trusted environments. This exposure to different value systems and social behavior is altering perceptions and the communal security in *known* truths or faiths. New telecommunications and information technology is accelerating this process of change. This is the first moment in history in which knowledge can truly be shared globally.

At first glance, this appears to be an exciting era of shared knowledge for the betterment of the species. Unfortunately, the world is a little more complex than that. Knowledge has always been seen as power. As with all power, it can be used for the good of many or the aggrandizement of the few. So knowledge has always been sought, and if not found it is invented, or the existing knowledge is altered, and then called faith. Throughout history, the proprietors of knowledge and the protectors of faith have fought to control and ration the dispersal of knowledge. With modern technology, such control has become increasingly difficult.

Recent history has provided many examples of how difficult it has now become to isolate or defeat external use of the power of knowledge. The first cracks in the Soviet empire became evident in East Berlin and then Hungary, as early as the 1950s. Worldwide, photographs and wireless kept the knowledge alive until it infected Poland and finally Russia itself. The growth of the new medium of television brought the Vietnam war into the living rooms of every American family. That knowledge changed the perceptions of millions. It not only brought the Vietnam war to an end, short of total victory—a new experience for the United States—but probably changed the United States forever. The capability of small video cameras to communicate directly with satellites makes it extremely difficult for those in authority to control the intended interpretation of events. This is as true for a Mississippi sheriff denying racism as for a Chinese warlord trying to deny Tienamen Square.

Old knowledge and traditional faith are under a barrage of attack from the new perceived knowledge.

From the perspective of history, this can be seen as a positive element in the development of thought and a driver in human endeavor. Yet we are creatures of habit and repeat all the old mistakes. A new stage has been reached, and little is considered of worth unless it can be labeled new. So thought must be atrophied until another stage has been accepted. The current era of "political correctness" could be cited as an example of this tendency. The fact that it should be rife in universities (the presumed centers of the search for knowledge) is disappointing but not really surprising. They are following historical precedent. Universities are usually in the forefront in protecting the faith and keeping new thinkers at bay.

Business Conflicts

The world of business is not immune to these changing perceptions and standards. There has been growing public disillusionment with the ethics of business. This is not surprising when profit can appear to be the only arbiter of business performance and the sheer greed of individual executives makes daily headlines. Business public relations seeks to cloak a purposeful fog over errors of judgment or downright incompetence or fraud. Could business apologists ever sink lower than the sheer obscenity of the annual report of Union Carbide that referred to its killing and maiming of thousands of people as the "incident at Bhopal"? As Hitler might have said, "the incident at Auschwitz should not be allowed to detract from the efficiency of the National Socialist state." These are exaggerated perceptions when applied to the behavior of the majority of companies, but they most certainly exist in today's society.

Environment of Uncertainty

All this change and uncertainty provides an ideal environment for the growth of false gods and gurus. Each introduction of a new utopia or technique helps to mold the perceptions of management and employees to develop a company culture. All too often, the flawed culture tends to obscure the fundamental purpose of the organization and bring about a general lack of focus. In such an environment, any change is seen as a threat rather than as an opportunity.

Sooner or later, disaster strikes the organization; or a new chief executive is appointed and the need for change is recognized. But by now, the company is late in relation to the market place; or the ego of the new executive is involved. As a result, a form of panic ensues and the change is often implemented as another revolution, or more accurately a managerial coup. As with military coups, this form of change brings disruption and confusion in its wake. There may well be a need for change, but in an era of uncertainty management tends to be satisfied with the quick fix. Again, managers are vulnerable to the prowling gurus and consultants. They will demonstrate a need to get rid of the dirty bathwater that obscures vision, but it is all too easy to throw out some hidden babies in the same process.

Putting Change Into Perspective

Organizations do not operate in an environment of their own making. They are part of, and to some extent subject to, the social and political environment of their time. Short-term judgments of those periods and their values are always interesting, if only because we were all part of them and were partly changed by them. However, these views are often suspect because historical judgment requires a perspective that is generally only gained over time. Some of the immediate judgments of the business climate and business values of the 1980s and early 1990s are seriously flawed.

Certainly, we have been through an era of change. The beginning of the realization of the technical opportunities for communication, the development of global competition, and the return of the concept of market-led economies are just a few such changes. At the same time, we have seen the collapse of communism and social collectivism. This has led to persistent questioning of any instance of the centralized interventionist role of government in the conduct of business. Even these questions are governed by our cultural experience and perspectives. Only a few years ago, I shocked a U.S. audience by the use of an ironic English sense of humor when I informed them that I found it interesting to be visiting the socialist state of Pennsylvania. I compared business conditions in their state with those in

Eastern Europe inasmuch as the liquor stores were all owned by the state of Pennsylvania. Not only that, but they exhibited all the behaviors I had observed in communist states. The liquor stores, rather than customer need, determined hours of operation and that they only sold liquor. In other words, if I wanted a tonic with my gin I now had to visit another shop to purchase the tonic. There are many such examples in the United States and Europe that can cloud objective views of business practices.

The populist view of the recent period as it applies to management is that the business climate has encouraged a new spirit of entrepreneurship but at the cost of a total degradation of business ethics. With a broader perspective, the validity of these assertions is questionable.

Consider first the view that we are in an era of innovation and entrepreneurship. Recently, we have seen the realization or application of a host of innovations and inventions of earlier eras. (We consider some of these in Chapter 8.) But in comparison with the nineteenth and early twentieth centuries in the United States and Europe, the real level of entrepreneurship realized in the 1980s and 1990s is puny indeed. There are aspects of information technology and biochemistry that could come close to earlier inventions. But in reality, can the innovation of today have any comparison with the impact of the discovery of the power of steam, electricity, coal, and oil? Within a relatively short period, we saw the introduction of the railroad, the automobile, electricity, radio, and the telephone. We have developed all these inventions in our lifetimes, but can we in any way claim that recent changes can equal or outdistance the impact of the changes of that period? Comparison of the two periods also demands discussion of how these changes were implemented and encouraged. This forms part of the argument for a return to commonsense management which occupies the third part of this book.

To some extent, the innovation of our period has been ephemeral and often reduced to mere manipulation of existing financial assets rather than generation of totally new assets. Asset stripping as a basis for mergers, bond manipulation, and many elements of "creative accounting" are indicative of this trend. Hopefully, the history of the late 1980s has taught us that recession is built on such shifting sands.

This general tenor may appear an overly negative assessment of the recent business contribution to our society. On the other hand, there is evidence that the easy judgment of what in Britain we call the "chattering classes" and some of the published pundits on the issue of business ethics has been equally wrong. There have been flagrant examples of corruption, fraud, and the complete absence of ethics in the conduct of business over recent periods. As a result, it has been easy to assume that greed is the key principle of modern business. But in fact a growing number of corporations and service organizations are putting responsibility to the community and a code of ethical conduct high on their agendas.

Professor Al Gini of Loyola University Chicago supports this recognition of a maturing approach by business executives. He edits a respected quarterly magazine entitled *Business Ethics,* which he says has a growing subscription list. He adds that "Any conference or workshop on business ethics has a ready audience of business executives." Voluntary development of the European Foundation for Quality Management (EFQM), in which major European corporations dedicated substantial funds and executive time to promoting quality standards and achievement for all, are evidence of this corporate responsibility. Again, international companies and organizations in the United States and Europe have collaborated easily to develop an agreed "Code of Conduct" in sharing information and the practice of benchmarking.

World-class companies operating in India, Southeast Asia, and Africa that were originally attracted by cheap labor are now taking a longer-term approach to their responsibilities to indigenous communities. From personal experience, I can attest to the work of Glaxo-Wellcome, Texaco, and Prudential Insurance in developing educational and community support operations that go far beyond their immediate need for basic skill training. All of these forward-thinking companies have become a little wary of providing lump-sum contributions to local communities. Somehow, such funds are quickly dispersed amongst self-appointed deserving citizens! Their support is now more often applied through skilled community leaders and teachers. In short, it is too easy to make quick judgments about worldwide irresponsibility of business in the global marketplace.

All organizations faced the pressure of the recession of the

1980s, but there were two schools of reaction. Some exhibited a ruthless disregard for the people they employed and the communities in which they operated. Others began to develop strategies that were heavily influenced by ethics and development of partnerships with their employees, customers, suppliers, and the community of which they are a part. (Those corporations are recognized later in the book.) Overall, there is reason for optimism as we look forward to the future working environment. However, once again in a historical perspective, this approach is not really new. We have only to return to a study of the great Quaker industrialists of the nineteenth century in both Britain and the United States to realize that there have always been responsible business leaders who viewed the management of resources in a much wider context than mere creation of profit and personal wealth.

The future corporation will play a larger, if not dominant, part in social development. Work organizations of the future need to put social goals on a parity with business goals. Executives and managers have to become more conscious of the needs and aspirations of their employees, the expectations of their customers, and their responsibility to the community and the environment. They must recognize that their stewardship of the organizations should also be for the benefit of future generations. So as not to see this as pie-in-the-sky aspirations for the future of business, we must understand one of the paradoxes of the changes taking place. The same convergence of technologies that has eliminated so many jobs and been at the heart of downsizing will in a relatively short time return a high level of power for the workforce. A high proportion of lost jobs relate to the old division between thinkers and doers. The future demands flexible use of knowledge and IT skills. The new workforce with those skills will not be so compliant as that of the past. This whole area of change is the subject of Chapter 12, "People." For now, it is clear that a lot of pebbles still need to be thrown.

Competing Philosophies

Perhaps we are more between philosophies than between gods. Most social institutions, including businesses, seem condemned to flirt with the philosophy of Plato before returning to the common sense of Aristotle. This may well be such a period, as we recover from the business gurus of recent years. The difference between these competing philosophies is a powerful undercurrent to the theme of this book. As individuals we have one major decision to make in life in as far as it provides a perspective for purposeful thinking: the choice between Plato and Aristotle.

The followers of Plato have the admirable intention of improving the world as quickly as possible. They identify a series of faults and weaknesses in the way society is organized or business operates. There is much validity in their observations, which are used to gain adherents. Like Plato, they retire to a back room and develop a new utopia or manifesto designed to put right all the perceived wrongs. Historically, this philosophical approach is at the root of socialist or communist (and sometimes rampant Socialist) solutions to the injustices of life. There is no harm in promulgating radical utopias as a spur to thought. Unfortunately, Platonic people are generally filled with zeal and a total commitment to the new faith. They are driven to see that the new utopia is imposed on the people (of course for the good of those same people) or on a business culture, with little or no argument accepted from those of "little faith" or the misguided who may be obstinately involved. In business terms, this philosophical approach has been applied to business through *prescribed* ways of implementing total quality management and business process reengineering. This is the dangerous area of the "four absolutes" prescribed by Philip Crosby, and the range of seven to twenty steps or habits of other gurus, which, they tell us, must be obeyed to achieve success.

Aristotle viewed life in a slightly different way. He was particularly interested in the organic or evolutionary way in which human institutions developed. Supporters of Aristotle could identify the same faults proclaimed by their Platonic brothers and sisters. *But* before rushing to develop a new utopia, they would pause for further thought. They would recognize that this same society that exhibited so many weaknesses also demonstrated many strengths. In other words, preceding periods had not been totally wasted and much had been achieved. Rather than demanding rapid or total change, Aristotelians are more likely to say how can we *conserve* what is good in our society or business and at the same time improve those facets that are bad. Of course, this evolutionary approach is not as exciting as the fresh and new solution to all the ills of the world. However, it is much closer to the real nature of people and organizations. The organic or evolutionary development of people and their progress as taught by Aristotle is a much surer philosophy for business.

There are many examples of businesses in the United States, Europe, and the Far East that exhibit this evolutionary approach, though they are unlikely to express their beliefs in these philosophical terms. I feature these businesses again and again as this book develops.

Culture and Values

That nothing is new is a pervading message of this book. Most of the ideas and concepts that I discuss are the result of the exercise of common sense proven by a legion of thinking managers. This is also true of the fundamental business ethics and the principles and values espoused by a number of corporations successful in the long run. There are, of course, mavericks; that is human nature. But almost without exception, the organizations that have grown and remained successful over extended periods have defined and maintained very clear values. In relation to the argument about Plato and Aristotle, a most interesting fact is that they are not necessarily the *same values*; in other words, there is no quick fix available in the values field. It is the presence of a value system that every member of the organization who wishes to remain part of the enterprise recognizes as the basis for action, rather than the specific value. The epitome of a world-class evolutionary organization that has relied on its strong value system to establish such supremacy is the world's largest consulting services firm, Arthur Andersen.

The modern values of Arthur Andersen have in the main been developed from the original pronouncements of their founder as far back as 1913. The overall flavor of this influence can be judged from his statement that "We will measure our contribution more by the quality of service rendered than by whether we make a good living out of it." But very few organizations successfully maintain the ethos of their founder over some nine decades. A key element in their continued success in the field is to be found in the importance they place on ensuring that the values of the *firm* are understood by every employee and potential partner.

Their educational center at St. Charles, Illinois (itself evidence to the proportion of revenue they devote to employee development) has a "culture center" that helps every student, and thus in time every partner, to take personal ownership of these values. Of interest to the theme of this book is that the values of Arthur Andersen are not by any means *soft* in the sense of most recent books advising organizations on developing value systems. Merit is a strong element in the firm's value systems; in other words, those who cannot reach the competence level and probably the work rate level of their colleagues do not long survive in Arthur Andersen. But another value is "stewardship," which places a duty on each generation of partners to revere their inheritance and to ensure that they pass on to the next generation an improved firm.

The power and evolutionary nature of the value systems of Arthur Andersen were tested in the period of the mergers of the leading accountancy and consulting firms in the 1980s. A possible merger between themselves and another giant was considered and investigated by both organizations. It would have created the preeminent worldwide force in the field of consulting organizations. The partners eventually decided not to pursue the negotiations because they feared a negative impact on the culture and core values of the firm. When the spate of other mergers had settled down, Arthur Andersen dropped from first to fifth place in the rankings of service firms. Yet within a decade they had regained their place as the leader. They have achieved their growth, in part, because they were not prepared to sacrifice their culture.

The values of Arthur Andersen have been consistently communicated throughout the firm to the extent that they are shared values forming the core of the firm's culture. These values provide a common focus that concentrates their people, training, methodologies, tools and techniques, and business processes and policies on meeting and exceeding the expectations of their clients. The firm's culture requires each individual to take ownership of the quality of service delivered. All their training and methodologies are directed toward empowerment of people to reinforce their client-first philosophy, expressed by the founder in the quote earlier. It is interesting to note in the context of this book that the principal goals for all categories of employees put empowerment first, followed by responsibility and innovation. These are not just time-serving aspirations. Arthur Andersen spends in excess of $500 million annually on training and development of its people and ensuring the permanence of its highly successful culture. Pause for a moment. Half a billion dollars is fairly substantial as total revenue, let alone as a figure for the education and training budget! But look at the results. The firm has nurtured *generations* of pebble throwers.

We return to the values of Arthur Andersen in Chapter 9, on purpose. In this chapter, we now turn to two companies that in their different ways demonstrate other facets of the evolutionary process.

Customer Focus

Two British companies, Marks and Spencer and J. Sainsbury, are prime examples of evolutionary companies that continuously succeed in every business climate. Both are also involved in the U.S. market. They are interesting in that both were formed in the last century and have continued to dominate their own sectors of the retail and distribution industry. Both have been largely owned and managed by descendants of the founding families, though recently there has been influence from outside the initial core. Their management concepts have been and are still based on the principles of continuous improvement. They have generally been ahead of their manufacturing brethren in early introduction of technology and leading management concepts. Indeed, their own management practices have encouraged introduction of the same concepts into their suppliers in food processing and clothing manufacture. It is worthwhile considering why these companies became and remained the leaders in their chosen fields.

First, retail and distribution is the most customer-focused of all industries. From the medieval marketplace, through Main

Street, and now to the great shopping malls, survival has depended on understanding the volatile expectations of customers. More than any other industry, it is dependent on the day-to-day decisions of customers. The changing face of the shopping market is part of the social history of our times. Old names disappear and new names arise. Gimbels, Lipton, and Woolworth's have gone or lost their dominance; Wal-Mart, Next, and The Body Shop are new names. Great fortunes have been made and lost by recognizing or missing a fundamental change in the market. The long-term winners work so hard at listening to their customers that they continuously improve and succeed.

Second, Marks and Spencer and J. Sainsbury were founded by entrepreneurs with great energy and vision. That is not the only reason for their enduring excellence, because over the same period other entrepreneurs with marketing vision have soared across the sky but eventually crashed to earth. The sustained competitive advantage of these two companies has been achieved by customer focus and adherence to their own value systems. In both cases, their values are deeper and wider than that of seeking a market opportunity.

The two companies have always understood their markets. As they expanded, they developed a culture that led their managers to continuously monitor these markets (or, more simply, listen to their customers) so that they were usually in a position to lead as customer perceptions changed. Above all, they understood the constraints of their businesses and the roles of people, technology, and processes in the organization of their companies. The vision of these company founders created highly successful cultures that were well communicated to successive generations of managers and workers. It is not a coincidence that Marks and Spencer, J. Sainsbury, and Arthur Andersen invest well above the norm in the development of their people.

A long while ago (1948), I shared student quarters with two Marks and Spencer management trainees. The memory of their commitment and obvious enjoyment in their work has remained ever since. Perhaps the most crucial lesson I learned from the experience was from the M and S educational approach of theory, practice, action. All of their students were introduced to an element of management theory in practice and were later given an assignment that ensured that they put an element of what they had learned into action. I make no apologies for featuring the company here; their progress has intrigued me ever since those student days.

Developing Markets

J. Sainsbury is a UK leader in the food supermarket segment and in recent years has successfully entered two other market segments. Its Homebase do-it-yourself sector has recently expanded with the acquisition of Texas DIY outlets to become the dominant force in that field. Now its "Savacentres," huge multifranchise hypermarkets, are to be seen across the United Kingdom and Europe.

Marks and Spencer is renowned worldwide for basic clothing stores. It is famed for quality (as opposed to luxury) clothes to suit everyone of whatever perceived social class or income. Winston Churchill and Margaret Thatcher may have patronized prominent tailors and couturiers, but it is reputed that their underpants and bras have been purchased from Marks and Spencer. Both Marks and Spencer and J. Sainsbury are noted for their quality and value for money. Both have always rejected the quick-fix promotion of business through gimmicks such as Green Stamps.

Marks and Spencer has moved successfully from clothing to food. The "Food Hall" additions to their main stores have been a major success and set standards for all their competitors. Unique choice, high quality, and reasonably priced prepared foods from M and S have been a staple content of suburban dinner parties. This move, however, was within the range of the company's core competencies.

The characteristics of the food and general clothing sectors of retail and distribution are relatively similar. The obvious similarity is that whatever happens, people will always need food and clothing; but it would be unwise to base a successful business on that premise alone. Tastes in specific foods and fashions in clothes are constantly changing. This demands intense management focus on the customer and a detailed knowledge of perceptible changes in buying patterns from area to area. It then requires a sophisticated distribution system to enable managers to react to those changes at just the right moment. Both companies have now reached a level of sophistication such that they know to the hour which of their hundreds of outlets have too few or too many cans of baked beans or panties of a specific size on their shelves. Knowledge is one thing, but communication, and empowerment of individual mangers to act, are essential parts of their successful cultures.

Even the best companies make mistakes. They can be successful in markets other than their original focus, although only in the case of markets that exhibit similar characteristics. When they stray from their managerial culture or core competencies, they face difficulties. Marks and Spencer's purchase and subsequent management of Brooks Brothers is a case in point. The two companies have totally different characteristics. They may both be in the clothing market, but semi-tailored clothing for the conservative "top market" has little relationship in management processes and practices to mass-produced underwear and jumpers. It has not been a happy marriage.

Management Practices

Marks and Spencer and J. Sainsbury have placed great emphasis on the education and training of their people. Both have usually been way ahead of their competitors in introducing and developing management practices and the latest techniques. A factor that has concentrated management attention on continuous improvement of their people and their business processes is the fact that both their market sectors are high-volume, rapidly moving, and low-margin businesses. In this environment, a penny—or even a fraction of a penny—saved per unit without sacrificing quality can make millions. These companies did not need the Japanese or quality gurus to concentrate their minds on the waste and hassle elements of internal quality.

In this context, Marks and Spencer was practicing total quality management long before it became fashionable. In 1961, the British Productivity Council produced a training film entitled "Right First Time." The advisers to the filmmakers were from Marks and Spencer, which was demonstrating how it achieved zero defects and practiced prevention through setting clear requirements at every stage of a process. This was seventeen years before Philip Crosby wrote *Quality Is Free,* in which he described the concept of getting it right the first time. Perhaps more to the point, M and S was describing a management approach that it had been developing since the 1930s.

Common Sense

Changing circumstances require new methods and even a reexamination of the values of an organization, but that is not the same as starting all over again or creating totally new gods. Most management fashions or the teachings of the latest business guru are, in truth, somewhat tardy reactions to changes that were long ago anticipated by the evolutionary companies. The impact of the gurus relies on the unfortunate fact of history that most organizations do not anticipate the future. The organizations face the inevitable results of their mindless management, and so time and again the latest book seems to portray revealed knowledge. This approach condemns business to periodic breakthrough steps to the new plateau, only to discover once again that they go on demonstrating their incompetence and lack of thought.

The evolutionary companies constantly apply practical common sense to the changing circumstances around them. Their people are trained to recognize those circumstances and empowered to react to changes. As a result, their progress is relatively smooth and shows few massive changes or reengineering. Their fundamental values are based on common sense rather than the worship of false gods. In Chapter 2, we examine some of the false gods that have tempted the foolish.

Questions for the Reader

Several chapters in this book contain a number of questions for the reader. They are to assist you in checking the arguments of the chapter with perceptions from your own experience:

1. Have you experienced "flavor of the month" changes that created upheaval but accomplished little?

2. Have you witnessed managerial decisions that appear to defy common sense?
3. Does your organization closely monitor the changing perceptions of your customers?
4. Have you been involved in radical change and been concerned that some important issues were ignored or overlooked?
5. Does your organization stay ahead of and take advantage of developments in technology?
6. Do you personally know and understand the values of your own organization?
7. Can you identify any examples of day-to-day business activities that are in conflict with those values?
8. Do you consider that your corporate office or senior management is too remote from the real issues of the business?

Chapter 2

False Gods

Man is quite insane. He wouldn't know how to create a maggot, and he creates Gods by the dozen.
Montaigne (1533–1592)

Our life is frittered away by detail . . . simplify, simplify.
Henry Thoreau (1817–1862)

When it is not necessary to change, it is necessary not to change.
Lucius Cary (1610–1643)

In the main, executives, managers, and other employees want to do a good job. There are some personal agendas, but generally they are united in that they want their company to be successful and respected. Yet despite this unity of attitude, organizations lose sight of the changing marketplace and are plagued with turf wars and adversarial relationships. The activities of business have become so enshrouded in an all-pervading fog that individuals are lost in a maze of procedures and other barriers to communication and action.

This chapter concentrates on the false gods of business and highlights their destructive effects on organizations. These can be summarized:

False Gods	*Destructive Effects*
⊙ Specialization	⊙ Creates a culture of "the thinkers and the doers" or "them and us"

False Gods	*Destructive Effects*
◉ The corporate office	◉ Removes decisions from the front line
◉ Profit	◉ Maximizes short-term profit; often sacrifices tomorrow
◉ Management assumptions	◉ Weaken strategic focus
◉ The finance department	◉ Its all-pervading power saps initiative
◉ Marketing myths	◉ Confuses the difference between marketing and selling
◉ The cost of training	◉ Leads to lack of investment in people; the cost of ignorance far exceeds the price for training
◉ The human resources department	◉ Line management abdicates its role in managing people
◉ Lawyers	◉ Stultify all decisions; desperate need to curb their influence
◉ Public relations	◉ Obscure the real purpose; the spin doctors of business
◉ Scientific management	◉ Rationalizes bad habits and sets them in concrete

The God of Specialization

The intriguing fact is that step by step the overcomplication of business has all been done on purpose in the name of enlightened management. It all started when Adam Smith and then Frederick Taylor and countless apostles demonstrated to businesspeople that if they divided major processes or work activities into a host of small specialized activities, they could achieve massive increases in productivity. They were proved right; the era of the craftsman ended and the era of mass production began.

The pioneers of modern industry and commerce were right at the time and in the conditions in which they promulgated their ideas. But some of the side effects of the new prescription were not recognized (or even deliberately ignored); and then conditions changed. The progress of technology; education; and the expectation of customers, employees, and society have since evolved to a stage that demands a reevaluation of the original theory.

One result of pursuing specialization has been the steady division of business operations and the people involved in them, both horizontally and vertically, that is, a vertical division between the thinkers and the doers and a horizontal division between specialized or departmental functions. Over time each division has created barriers to communication and understanding of how the business is operating. The phenomenon of us versus them is wider than the division between managers and workers. On the people front, the confrontation is layered between boss and subordinate at every level. On the activity front, functional departments have become fortresses to be defended at any cost. Ultimately, in this environment the organization views its customers and suppliers as combatants to be subdued.

All the divisions of specialization have contributed to deterioration in human relations in the business environment. We return to this aspect of business history later, but in this context let us note that it leads to destruction of communication upon which purpose, focus, and timely action must depend.

Perhaps the most destructive division of all has been that between the thinkers and the doers. Modern technology has steadily automated the doer jobs and increasingly demanded thinking workers for its management. There is recognition of this changing need for skilled workers, but in industry old attributes die hard. The expectation is that the gap must be filled with new workers who have these inherent skills. The existing workforce can continue to hang up their brains with their overcoats as they enter the facility. The gods of specialization have still to be assuaged—but the price is high.

The Gods of Corporate Office

As the channels of communication and action have become more complex and time consuming, the thinkers have taken the easy option and employed more and more people to advise them. These advisers are expected to organize the disparate elements of the business so that the executives can concentrate on the five-year plan. The advisers are organized into staff groups who exercise power and control on behalf of (and often instead of) the executives and senior managers rather than the actual customer of the business. As the eyes, ears, and voice of management, they serve to reinforce the separation between management and worker. Even more: This trend has divided management from the customer and the real issues of the marketplace and actually prevented managers from realizing the purpose of the organization.

In most businesses today, a substantial proportion of managers and advisers have little or no contact with the customer. At the same time, they also have little or no contact with the people who make products or deliver services. They live in corporate offices (the chateaux of Chapter 1) and spend their working hours with other managers or "members of the staff." They are far removed from changing customer perceptions, the "insignificant" problems of the workers, and the reactions of difficult customers. Too often, the energy of corporate staff is expended on jockeying for political position and extending their privileges rather than on improving the business. Management becomes immersed in pointless detail, and the business is slowly frittered away.

In this environment few take risks; therefore opportunities are missed. Fear of not being able to see the forest for the trees has misled many business leaders into believing that the competitive forest is composed of mighty oaks, when in truth it is merely populated with brittle fir saplings. The business is steadily atrophying.

Executives, isolated in their chateaux, have high thresholds of pain. The company has to lose its major customer, be faced with a hostile takeover bid, or face a major cash-flow crisis before the executives really react and their attention is wholly engaged. Then all hell breaks loose, and special task forces are formed or consultants called in to solve this major problem. All the way down the pyramid, varying levels of managers have their own thresholds of pain that motivate action. Down among the workforce, no one is allowed to have a threshold of pain (though they live in pain all day long). They are not empowered to set up task forces, employ consultants, or gain the attention of managers who control the resources. As a result, they keep fixing thousands of little problems for customers but are never able to dedicate the time or resource to get at the root cause to prevent them recurring. In reality, whatever way gurus describe empowerment, the real issue is to give the workers involved with day-to-day issues permission to breach all the thresholds of pain.

The God of Profit

Profit is not an ugly word; it is a reasonable objective for any business. However, concentration on short-term profit objectives is an ugly process for which in the long run many businesses pay a horrendous price. The traditional short-term measure of the salesperson—"You are only as good as last month's figures"—is now applied to the whole business. It is the wrong way to achieve sales success; it is disastrous to the whole business. The false god of maximizing short-term profit usually sacrifices tomorrow.

To some extent, this attitude is almost forced upon management by the pressures emanating from the stock market and large institutional investors. Yet it has also become a deeply ingrained habit in many corporations. It is particularly noticeable in international assignments. Aspiring top executives are often sent to manage overseas operations or "colonies" of the corporation before being offered a major corporate office. Their overseas "package" includes strong revenue or profit objectives as a corollary to exciting payment and benefit packages. These are relatively short-term packages, usually of two years' duration. The executives tend to follow a number of similar "ex-patriots," all with the same short-term objectives. Great people at many international corporations have been held back by this management practice. It is very frustrating working locally with executives tasked in this manner and in the last six months of their sojourn. Every decision is prefaced by the question "How will this impact *my* revenue or profit objectives?" rather than the real merit of the options available.

World-class evolutionary companies do not make profit

their primary objective. Management concentrates on the process of delighting their customers. They know that in this way profit automatically follows. This is not a late-twentieth-century concept. The Hindu scriptures of the *Gita* teach the individual to work at the processes of life rather than focus primarily on the results. It is also an element in the teaching of W. Edwards Deming, the quality guru. There are some negative aspects of this approach, but it is worth noting that successful corporations such as Toyota, Virgin, and Sony are highly profitable organizations although profit is not their main business objective. Evolutionary companies work toward holistic objectives centered around the customer, business processes, and the innovative potential of their people.

Corporate Distortion

Specialization and executives' relish for reorganizing the management structure have succeeded in making the operation of business complicated. In fact, business is simple; a host of mindless managers have only made it appear complex. For example, look at the stratified layers of vice-presidents who populate the corporate chateaux. Viewed from a detached satellite, only three management positions can really be considered to oversee a strategic process and therefore matter in the business process. Figure 2-1 illustrates the key business processes and key executives.

● *Customer focus*: the head of marketing, who is responsible for defining customer needs and expectations and then designing products and services to delight the customers
● *Company strategy*: the chief executive, who is responsible for determining the strategic direction of the business, resolving the conflict inherent between the other two positions, and organizing resources and support
● *Delivery*: the head of production or operations, who is responsible for developing capability and then delivering the product or service to the customer

All other functions or departmental heads are only there to support these processes. This original rock-steady triumvirate of

Figure 2-1. The key business processes.

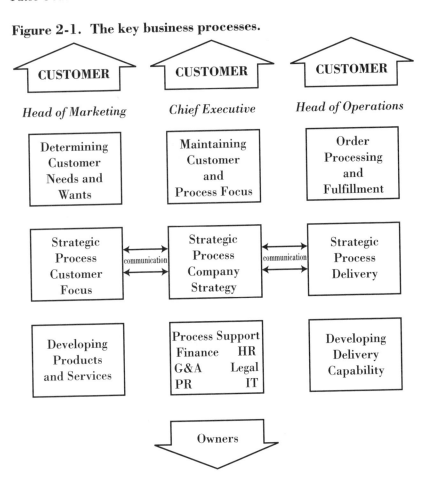

management based on the purpose of business has been distorted. Other functions have been allowed to unbalance the simple triangle. This has been to the detriment of long-term decision making and management of organizations. The clouding of these simple principles has led to the decline of many organizations.

This can be illustrated as a process which has continued over the years, having the following tendencies:

⦿ The rise in the power of financial vice-presidents in the 1950s and 1960s has led to an obsession with Wall Street, quarterly results, and short-term financial thinking. Financial controllers dominate corporate thinking and much of the activity of the business. Perhaps an even more pernicious tendency is the succession factor. Increasingly, new chief executives are selected from the financial arena.

⊛ The rising influence of HR directors in the 1970s has steadily sapped management's will to manage people.

⊛ Since the 1980s, we have seen the growing influence of lawyers across the whole business spectrum. They have spawned the fear of litigation that inhibits so much entrepreneurship.

⊛ Now the spin doctors or public relations specialists are seeking a seat at the business decision-making table.

These and other tendencies have created habits of thought that are obscuring the true purpose of the key processes of business and public-sector organizations. None of these functions represent key business processes or are actually essential to the strategic purpose. A moment's consideration of how businesses start, and indeed how most successful small businesses operate, makes this point clear. These functions just do not exist in a small business; when skill or advice is required in these areas it is almost always sourced outside the business. We consider the answer to this issue in Chapter 9.

Management Assumptions

Further examination of Figure 2-1 challenges a number of assumptions that are often taken for granted in business organizations:

⊛ *Selling is a subprocess of the main business process of delivery rather than an element in the marketing process.* In many businesses, the words *marketing* and *sales* are treated as synonyms, but applied thought indicates the dangers of relying on selling for market intelligence. Most salespeople are tasked and often heavily incentivized to sell the company's *existing* product or service range. They are positively discouraged from soliciting views on what changes the customer would like in the product. Conversely, balanced marketing decisions would be corrupted by the emotional element involved in selling and obtaining *immediate* revenue.

◉ *Order processing, billing, and management of receivables are part of the delivery process.* But many companies place these processes under the control of the finance or central administrative function. In essence, this is because cash flow is seen as a key financial issue. It may be, but the assumption that the finance department can solve it demonstrates lack of knowledge of processes. The queries or errors in billing that lead to most overdue receivables stem from miscommunication between the customer and delivery, or between the administrative function and delivery, or both. The process or team that is responsible for delivery should also be responsible for billing and collection. There is then a reasonable chance that the real parties to the transaction would know what they are talking about and thus quickly resolve any differences. In those companies that take this course, the level of overdue receivables is dramatically lower. In addition, customer-supplier relations are happier because there are fewer frustrations.

◉ *Research and product development are part of the customer-driven marketing process.* It is just possible to make a case in some specialized industries for so-called pure research, but the argument is at best tenuous. Business history is littered with examples of pure-research "sinkholes" for corporate resources. A controlled contribution to external research institutions is a viable option to keep in touch with the cutting edge of research. The time it takes for *breakthrough* scientific discoveries to become practical applications is so long and expensive that it is beyond the resources and decision perspectives of almost every business. Active business should concentrate on directed research and development to meet perceived needs through *known* concepts.

◉ *The departments of finance, human resources, legal, public relations, and management information systems are critical to the health of the organization.* This is a dangerous assumption that has grown in credence in corporate chateaux. They are not; they exist only to support the key processes. This raises some major issues for management and control of organizations. For example, a large number of the procedures and controls that regulate or limit the activities of the key processes emanate from these subprocess groups. We pursue this argument further on, but in the immediate context it is worth asking the question, "What on earth does the finance department have to do with the purchasing function or establishment of marketing or manufacturing budgets?!"

As we continue to examine these issues, we realize that focusing on the purpose of the organization is the key to evolutionary change. The chief executive is charged with resolving the natural differences in competing needs for resources that come from the key processes and thus determine the strategic direction of the organization. The three strategic processes depicted in Figure 2-1 all have arrows directing their focus to the customer. The chief executive alone has an arrow to indicate that part of his or her focus must also be on the owners. In this context, the word *owners* can mean individual owners, institutional and general public shareholding, or elected government bodies. The CEO's role as well has been compromised by the too easily accepted assumptions of business.

These corporate assumptions have evolved as successive generations of management launch specialized initiatives or meekly accepted the current fad or false god. Today these assumptions are now embedded in the culture of the organization.

As we examine the effect of following false gods we should bear in mind, in the social language of today, that the business body may need therapy and detoxification rather than radical surgery. The paradox of dramatic change is that the methods used for implementation are more likely to deepen the divisions and barriers to communication that caused the problems in the first place.

The Gods of Finance

Over the last fifty years, the power of the financial department has risen beyond all reason. This is linked to short-term profit objectives but has permeated corporate culture to an even greater extent. It has become a major impediment to success in a high proportion of companies.

Finance departments feel comfortable in risk-free environments, and so they seek to eliminate risk. A series of financial controls, regulations, and audits are issued. With each new control or procedure, the finance department reduces individual responsibility, accountability, and the sense of ownership that drives leaders. Some leaders break through, but for too many all initiative is stifled.

Looked at with a process perspective, it hardly seems possible that so many companies would allow the financial staff to accrue so much power. Without demur, it is now accepted that it is the role of finance to set the parameters for operational budgets, departmental goals, and the prime measures of ascertaining performance. The fact that the financial controllers have little or no knowledge of the processes involved in delighting customers doesn't seem to matter. The chief financial officer shall be called God.

I first encountered this aspect of corporate life some thirty years ago. I had been appointed to set up a new operation to win government business. It was not an easy task, but I was excited by the challenge. It quickly became apparent that I needed people with skills that were not readily available in the company. I submitted a budget for resources that was about double what finance had allocated; not surprisingly, both finance and operational superiors were a brick wall. Yet the new operation was almost certain to fail without these resources. In the end, the only way to gain the budget to provide operational freedom was to propose and accept a financial results goal for the first year that was nearly three times more than my own objective assessment of what was possible. It was clear that it would take at least two years to reach that level of performance.

In negotiating with the finance department, I gambled that I would not be sacked at the end of the first year for failing to make the goals. I also accepted that I would not receive an incentive bonus for the year. The team was held together by clearly dividing the task into a "year of preparation" and a "year of achievement." In the event, there was some derision from peer groups at the end of the first year when the new group achieved only 40 percent of the false financial goal, but in the second year it did surpass all expectations. One of my proudest possessions is a pewter tankard from the team, inscribed "The Year of Achievement."

There is nothing unique in this experience. Countless managers have met this situation over and over again. Finance could feel that the books were balanced by providing an increased budget to meet an increased financial goal. Little account was taken of operational experience that could demonstrate that both the original budget and the amended target made operational nonsense. In such an environment, where there should be trust there is duplicity. But the real tragedy is that in most cases managers are not in the position to take risk, and so opportunities are lost.

Financial Measurement

The use of monthly and quarterly financial results as the arbiter of business success can result in a short-term focus that permeates the whole organization. This alone can restrain rather than release people's potential. There is nothing wrong with short-term measurement per se, but there is an issue about what we are measuring. In successful companies, measurement is often the outward sign of inward grace. Companies should be continuously sampling or measuring the performance of their key business processes to determine (1) what their capability is, (2) that the processes are in control, and (3) that the degree of variation between measures is natural to the process. This enables managers to manage the process rather than concentrating on managing the results. Process measurement indicates what *is* happening; financial measurement is a snapshot that *may* indicate what *has* happened. Management action based on snapshot financial figures can lead to knee-jerk reactions predicated by what they think might have happened. Process measurement gives early warning of trends and much more confidence in the long-term capability of the processes that produce the results. Process measurement allows managers to concentrate on reducing variation, which will improve performance.

An example from process measurement makes the point of the danger of relying on short-term financial measurements. Figure 2-2 illustrates a trend chart used to ensure that a process

Figure 2-2. Trend chart using process measures.

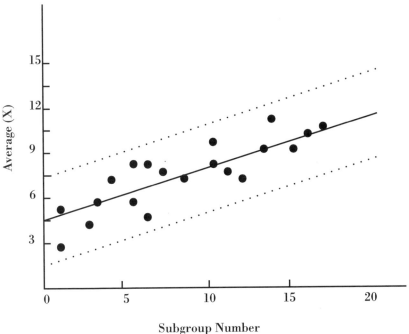

Subgroup Number

expected to produce a trend remains "in control." The dots represent the average of a series of sample measurements. The managers of this process understand the concept of variation, so they use a combination of sampling techniques and proven mathematics to determine the range of variation in results that they should expect. This determines what are called the upper control limit (UCL) and the lower limit (LCL) or band of variation. As long as the samples remain within these control limits and tied to a defined pattern, the manager knows that the process is in control within the limits of its capability and can thus predict its performance over time.

Using exactly the same chart of Figure 2-2 in Figure 2-3, but removing the control and capability indicators, we substitute process measures with financial measures. Now the center line represents the *budgeted* monthly revenue performance figures. The dots now represent a snapshot end-of-month financial picture. What is the likely management reaction to the recorded result at the end of month one—or even more so at the end of

Figure 2-3. Trend chart using finance measures.

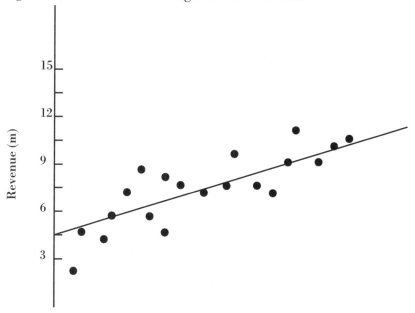

month three? It is: "Hell, we're more than two million below plan—do something!" Yet we happen to know, because of our measured knowledge of the processes, that the business is wholly in control and likely to meet its annual objectives. But in attempting to "do something," many management teams resort to short-term tampering with process and send it totally out of control. Typical tampering actions are immediate cost cutting, product price reductions or increases, reduced or increased advertising, and many other "action this day" responses that have little relation to what is actually happening at the sharp end.

None of the above is intended to demonstrate that accountants and other financial people are wicked destroyers of business "for they know not what they do." Rather, the key business process owners have allowed themselves to become besotted with the implication of financial figures. In some cases, this stems from fear of demonstrating a lack of "numeracy." Some potentially great operational managers have been held back because of a feeling that they were not wholly numerate. (An interesting aside: in reality it is often the executives with a financial background who could be accused of lack of numeracy; they have little or no understanding of statistics and such techniques as statistical process control.) The financial department has an important role to play in supporting and advising operations. But when all is said and done, the financial operations of most companies are not a key business process, and they most certainly should never be allowed to become the predominant influence on corporate strategy.

The Cost of People

In the language of business-speak, people are now popular despite (or perhaps because of) the fact most businesses are trying to get rid of them. No chairman's annual statement would be complete without the phrase "our people are our greatest asset." As Tom Peters has pointed out, the rest of the annual report belies that statement. All photographs of executives name them while everyone else is referred to as "a supervisor" or "one of our engineers"; they do not matter enough to be named. But the word *asset* is interesting in the current business financial environment. The accountants have defined labor as an operating cost. If people were defined as a capital cost and asset, they might be better maintained and developed. In current parlance, machines are more important assets than people.

The majority of executives still have to learn that the price of educating their staff is substantially lower than the cost incurred by their ignorance. This disparity grows rapidly as skill and knowledge become the determinants in business. Currently, the proportion of the annual operating budget allocated to education and training is derisory. At any hint of recession or weakening results, even this low allocation is one of the first areas for reduction.

The level of investment in education and training of all employees, including temporary staff, is one of the major contrasts between the successful evolutionary companies and the typical organization staggering from one "October revolution" to another. The very best are now exceeding an annual average of twenty days per employee. Many Japanese companies exceed thirty days per employee, but there are some difficulties in direct comparison as to what constitutes education and training. The majority of businesses in the West are satisfied with about five days per employee.

The visionary companies have always invested heavily in developing their people. I was facilitating a retreat of senior executives at one of our featured companies, discussing their key business issues. One executive highlighted the need to invest more in educating their people. I queried the reason for such a priority, because I knew that the company was way ahead of most and was investing millions of dollars per annum in this area. The reply was illuminating: "John, you do not understand, we spend that on training them to be technically the best in the world; we do not spend enough on educating them to be the best people and to be innovative leaders." The quotation admirably illustrates what should be meant by saying "our people are our greatest asset."

In this context, the British management writer Charles Handy makes an interesting point in arguing about the minimum wage. A strategy of keeping the costs of labor and training as low as possible was never a good long-term strategy. Management expects little and as a result gets little. If you pay people more, then there is an urgent need to get more out of them. Companies would be forced to educate and train their people to maximize their potential contribution.

The Gods of HR

Despite the underfunding of training, concern with the people issues in business management has reached significant proportions. The rise in influence of the human resources or personnel departments is indicative of this movement. It is also true, particularly in Europe, that the HR department has grown in status because of increased government employment legislation. Unfortunately, in practice this new focus has been a double-edged sword in many corporations.

On the positive side, the HR specialists are ostensibly interested in people and have some understanding of the behavioral sciences and other aspects of what is sometimes called the soft side of management. HR departments generally encourage more emphasis on:

- Education, training, and management development
- Motivation and empowerment of people
- Communication and feedback
- Teamwork, quality improvement, and similar initiatives

On the negative side, HR departments exhibit all the dangers of specialization. Once upon a time, personnel director was a general management post, often on a rotational basis for key executive development. Many people in the department would have line experience. Today, the lead role is almost always held by a professional HR specialist. Secure in their unrivaled knowledge of the concepts of people management, they win the power to develop and implement personnel policies, procedures, and practices for the whole organization. This can act to the detriment of any innovative culture when the HR department has overall responsibility for:

- *Recruitment*: HR drafts the advertisements and kindly "saves management time" by sifting through employment applications to arrive at a final interview short list. They often sit in on these final interviews; though in fairness they do not usually make the final decision, most of the time harassed managers do not really question the HR short list. Once the decision is made, HR then issues the hiring letter and organizes induction and training. *The result:* The business steadily becomes populated with "safe" people who made the short list. In other words, HR decides who is unlikely to give management (or HR) any problems. The new recruits won't challenge the organization or act as unwanted stimuli with a different perspective. In essence, line management has abdicated its responsibility and fallen at the first hurdle.

- *Pay and performance*: HR becomes responsible for pay, performance measurement, and grievance structures. Soon HR naturally becomes responsible for all pay and grievance negotiations. *The result:* Management abdicates responsibility for managing people in their business processes. Negotiating points become generalized and remote from the "action." This tendency played a large part in the disastrous growth of union power in the 1960s and 1970s in the United Kingdom, when all negotiations were centralized and captured on "sound bite" television. The union's "right" to negotiate on behalf of employees became enshrined and management became "represented" in a similar fashion. This whole process was eventually reversed by Margaret Thatcher and her stringent trade union legislation.

⦿ *Education and training*: HR involvement has generally been beneficial in this area, but there are some dangers in the specialist approach. HR usually determines the content and form of the training curriculum. The problem arises when the HR specialist has a particular bee in the bonnet and it takes precedence over real business needs. *The result:* Line management has a tendency to select training for its subordinates from an available menu rather than determining the process needs for people development.

The Awesome Gods of Law

Perhaps the most pernicious trend in business over recent decades has been the increasing influence of the lawyers and the corporate legal department. The mythical businessperson's reaction to a newsflash stating that six hundred lawyers are feared drowned in a convention cruise ship disaster, "Sounds like a good start to me," is a natural reaction. The real point of the joke is that such macabre humor works because it expresses a shared truth. Allegedly, there are now more attorneys in the United States than in the rest of the world put together. Western Europe now appears to want to play catch-up. Perhaps a solution is for the president to sponsor a new Lend Lease Agreement whereby the United States would transfer a substantial number of lawyers to Eastern Europe and China, which actually *need* them.

Attorneys have no role to play in the essential processes of business, yet our corporations are dominated by them. We have reached a position where it now seems impossible to have any meaningful business meeting or negotiation without the presence of attorneys. As a young businessman I never forgot my first exposure to this phenomenon, as long ago as 1960. I wanted to franchise a specialist software package through IBM service centers in the United States. Through persistence and naïvete, I had managed to arrange a meeting with Tom Watson at the old World Trade Center near the United Nations. Four other people were at the meeting; to my amazement, I found that three of them were attorneys. I remonstrated that I didn't deal with lawyers until after agreement had been reached with principals. It is perhaps needless to say that this particular Englishman did not get the IBM business! But that was not the environment in which business was conducted in even earlier years, including those periods of explosive and successful business growth in the United States. In the main, business leaders discussed the pertinent issues based on their marketing, operational, and funding constraints. They reached agreement and then *instructed* their attorneys to draw up contracts based on that agreement. Most of the enduring business giants were founded on that basis.

Too often today, the all-pervading presence of the legal eagle obfuscates the simple principles of business. The successful deal used to be one that was good for both parties; now it appears to be one that steals a legal march on the other party.

From a business perspective, there is an interesting aspect in the position of the law relative to the normal business relationship between customer and supplier. In less than thirty years, that relative position has been almost completely reversed. In this area, common or case law was based primarily on the concept of *caveat emptor*, or let the buyer beware. But since the advent of global competition and Ralph Nader, the perception of the customer and the law has had to change. The consumer is now organized and wields political clout. The legislature, ever mindful of consumer votes, has responded with a host of consumer-oriented legislation. This trend has been combined with the formation of many new regulatory bodies and quasi politically correct bodies ever eager to constrain business. The legal basis for the key relationship in business is now "let the seller beware." This *volte-face* is not necessarily wrong, but it is different.

This fundamental alteration in the legal concepts that govern business has not fazed the attorneys. As they may well explain, their role is to argue the law, not to make it. Confusing changes in legislation open further fronts for their nimble minds. On one front, they exist to protect the business entrepreneur from the real purport of the law by skillful use of fine print. As a result, protection of the environment, delighting of customers, and the status of employees and other stakeholders is now hedged about with legal jargon. On another front, the fee-conscious attorney can encourage consumers, business associates, employees, and every conceivable environmental group to find legal precedents with which to further lambaste business.

On the surface, the beleaguered executive has little defense; so she or he hires yet more attorneys. The list of those who must be accommodated in the chateau expands, and business apes the national bureaucracy. Just as the UK Navy has more admirals than major warships, so corporate headquarters ends up with more legal assistants than they have meaningful contracts. And of course, now that there are so many lawyers aboard they must be properly represented in corporate decision making. The Gods of Law have created a purposeful fog around the process of decision making.

Somebody, somewhere has to call a halt to this mindless trend. We consider some solutions in Chapter 10.

The Insidious Gods of PR

Another growing influence within the corporate chateau is the public relations or communications department. PR consultants are not by definition clever exponents of marketing mumbo jumbo. They are mainly dedicated to representing the business and its products in the best possible light to aid success. In today's complicated society, marketing and promotion demand a whole series of skilled practitioners. Therein lies the problem.

Business has come to rely on these specialists' knowledge of the marketplace media and their perceived creativity. But the growing influence of the spin doctors is now reaching such a dimension that it is in danger of clouding purposeful vision and decision making. Executives are becoming enmeshed in the new language of "our visual image" and sound bites.

A personal example illustrates the issue. In a television interview, I was asked to nominate my favorite airline. I responded Virgin Atlantic and Emirates. The interviewer pushed for my favorite American airline, to which I replied Delta. That was the kiss of death because on my next two flights, both with Delta, I faced a series of minor but annoying faults in services. At the completion of the second flight, I noticed a Delta advertisement explaining the difference between performance and expectation. The billboard showed an airplane emblazoned with the Delta logo soaring into azure blue skies. The visual image was supported by the caption "We love to fly, and it shows!" This irate passenger exclaimed aloud "It sure does" and immediately wrote to the chief executive of Delta Airlines. The purport of the letter was "when you have stopped falling in love with your airplanes, please fall in love with your customers." As one might expect, this only produced a gushing letter from the PR department. It was along the lines of "We are delighted that our customers take the trouble to write to us . . . this was an isolated incident and we are certain that it will not happen again. . . . Regarding your comments on our logo we are delighted, etc. . . . But our research shows that the slogan has received a very positive response from our customers. . . ." A polite if not very helpful response.

Some period later, a short letter arrived from the Delta chief executive. Following a polite response to the original letter, the executive said, "I am not certain that you are right, but it will certainly be discussed with our agency." Some months later, the Delta slogan changed to "You'll love the way we fly"—a reversal of the original "adman" projection of the company to one centered on the customer. It recognizes that the purpose of an airline is not to fly airplanes but to move people by air. This change may well have been a complete coincidence, but I am delighted to confirm that all my recent flights with Delta have met or exceeded expectations.

The point of the story is that PR and advertising consultants are only there to advise how to project the vision decided upon by the *executives who run the business*, not the reverse. As I've said before about other functions, the communications department is not an essential process of business.

The God of Scientific Management

The concepts of specialization promulgated by Adam Smith and later by Frederick Taylor, the latter in his 1911 book *The Princi-*

ples of Scientific Management, have reigned supreme for most of this century. They are now found wanting. Evolutionary companies have risen from those methodologies, but many organizations are only just finding out that they need to change management behavior. Unfortunately, the drivers of revolutionary change concentrate on changing *other* managers' behavior rather than their own.

The first application of these principles resulted in the command, control, and compliance practices of management that are now largely rejected by thinking managers. To some extent, this is due to a changed environment that requires skilled workers (who are much less likely to be compliant), and to a broader definition of the word *scientific* as applied to management. Taylor's use of the word in relation to productivity and efficiency is now seen as overly mechanistic. Integration of aspects of the behavioral sciences has been an important influence in this change of perspective.

In fairness to the pioneers, in the enthusiasm to prove them wrong their overall views have been traduced in recent years, as this quotation from Adam Smith indicates: "The man whose life is spent in performing simple operations has no occasion to exert his understanding, or to exercise his invention in finding out expedients for difficulties which never occur. He naturally loses, therefore, the habit of such exertion and generally becomes as stupid and ignorant as it is possible for a human creature to become." That doesn't sound as if Smith *wanted* the workers to hang up their brains along with their caps when they entered the factory.

Management cultures still differ widely, but most now agree that Taylor's theories are no longer applicable to today's work environment. At least this is true in theory, but unfortunately many management practices are still anchored in traditional behaviors. We find it very difficult to change the daily small habits of a lifetime. They atrophy and prevent continuous evolutionary change until the pressure explodes and the corporation is faced with some form of revolution. Theory is accepted and managers learn that a participative style is better suited to achieving competitive performance. The same manager then *tells* subordinates how they are about to participate and practice teamwork. We preach participation but practice command and control and seem a little surprised that the workers do not comply. Some potential approaches to tackling this issue are examined in Chapter 12.

Questions for the Reader

You can get some indication of the false gods at loose in your own business by considering the following questions:

1. Do you ever feel that your opinion doesn't really count?
2. Do you find yourself in conflict with other specialist departments?
3. Do you feel that corporate headquarters really doesn't know what is happening in the field?
4. Can you identify opportunities that have been missed because of short-term financial considerations?
5. Do you believe that you have had a fair opportunity to influence and determine your operating budget?
6. Do you feel free to recruit and manage the people you need to accomplish your tasks?
7. How many days of education and training will you receive this year?
8. What part do you play in selecting your development and training?
9. Are you ever faced with "legal" clauses or elements of the contract that defy common sense in your relationship with customers?
10. Do you feel that the company makes promises in its advertising or public relations that are not truly representative of what you perceive the company has to offer?
11. Do you ever fall back into old habits that you know to be counterproductive?

Chapter 3

Entrenched Fads

Beware of false prophets, which come to you in sheep's clothing, but inwardly they are ravening wolves.

St. Matthew, The New Testament

Vain wisdom all, and false philosophy

Paradise Lost, John Milton (1608–1674)

The trouble with most management techniques is that they concentrate on only one facet of the management process. They are
often implemented by enthusiastic apostles with an uncritical belief that they represent a management breakthrough or a magic
cure-all. There is never time to consider how these techniques
or approaches are to be integrated with or replace existing procedures. Being a fad, the technique allows nothing to get in the
way of instant implementation. Doubters are derided as "ye of
little faith" or as traditionalists who are "past their shelf date."
All of this creates conflict and resistance throughout the organization. In some cases, the specific concept or technique is by its
very nature an agent of conflict, fear, and resistance. Management by objectives and unthinking application of most performance appraisal systems fall into this category. Some more recent
arrivals such as "empowerment" are in danger of being prosti-
tuted, thus creating even more confusion.

This chapter concentrates on some influential fads that have
dominated management thinking over a considerable period
with long-term consequences for organizations. These ap-

element of peer pressure and the desire of not wanting to let the team down, there is an essential truth buried in this behavior. There are too many variables, unforeseen events, and issues involved that are outside the control of the individual for anyone to willingly accept high or assigned goals. When the goal is also related to pay or survival, the pressure to seek a low goal is even greater. This element of fear associated with goal setting has fueled many trade union disputes. On the other hand, a team may feel that it has a wider scope of skills, experience, and tasks within the process to enable its members to handle the variation.

What actually happens during implementation of MBO is a companywide conspiracy to agree on soft objectives that everyone can meet, objectives that can thus be ignored. As recently as 1995, I was involved with a major corporation that maintained an MBO department (!), studiously developing MBO forms and charts, all to be meticulously deployed and completed at budget time. Every manager and supervisor agreed and signed for the objectives in his or her area of responsibility and then promptly forgot all about them until the following year. In such an environment, no one is accountable—and everyone *knows* that to be true; yet they all maintain the MBO charade. Using their common sense, people know that MBO objectives are useless because they bear no relation to the actual processes of work that have to be managed to accomplish goals.

The process diagram in Figure 3-1 illustrates the issue. An objective set for an individual manager using MBO is most likely to relate to the accumulated outcome of many outputs of the work process in which they are involved. Clearly, the outputs of this process must meet the requirements of the process customer, who may be internal or external. These requirements may also be included in the individual's objective. But here is the rub. For the process to continuously perform so that the objective is met, a number of other requirements must also be met. These requirements are probably outside the control, or even the influence, of the individual who has been set the output objective.

An example demonstrates the point. In a manufacturing process, the line manager sets a production objective for which his or her people are accountable. But why should they accept the objective when they have no responsibility for the purchasing department, which has been set an objective to buy the

Figure 3-1. Setting objectives.

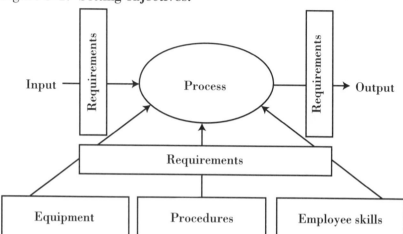

cheapest materials? How does the line manager then ensure that the supplier delivers the right quality materials to meet the input requirements of the manufacturing process? Again, does the line manager also have the power to ensure that all the people involved have the requisite skills and have been properly trained, that all the procedures are in place and are relevant, and finally that the manufacturing equipment is suitable and fully maintained? In most cases, the answer is no!

Setting objectives, goals, and requirements is much more complex than MBO ever envisaged when applied to individuals. However, it can be quite simple if the team of people involved understand the concept of processes and then agree on goals in an integrated manner. Of course the essential lesson is that the organization needs to spend its time and resources to greater effect in measuring processes rather than individual people.

Performance Appraisal Systems

Performance appraisal systems are one of the control mechanisms in the scientific management concept of command, control, and compliance. However considerately these systems are implemented, the essential element remains: boss evaluating subordinate to determine reward or punishment.

In many systems, there is yet another element of control over the bosses' evaluations. The HR department, which knows nothing about the individual's performance, issues parameters that determine the number or percentage of people who can be evaluated as excellent, good, average, and below average. In other words, the evaluations are slanted before they begin, which is immensely unfair to the people concerned. When will management ever learn that any evaluation system based on these principles must statistically decree one-half the people as above average and the other half as below average, *however* well they perform?

In this situation, the HR department may put the leader of a dedicated team in an impossible situation. The manager has taken great care to select or recruit the very best in each discipline to create a high-performance team. But now she or he is supposed to implement the divisive policy of selecting only a small percentage as excellent. The best companies have developed totally new approaches to rewarding team members (which we consider in Chapter 12), but the majority persist with inappropriate personnel policies.

Deming and many others have demonstrated in their writing and consulting why this seemingly reasonable system or measurement device is in fact destructive. Some of the arguments are rooted in the issues discussed earlier under MBO, but to summarize the main points, performance appraisal:

- Is focused on individuals without reference to the performance of the processes in which they work
- Encourages the individual rather than the team or group of people with whom the individual works
- Ignores variations in processes, systems, and other people outside the individual's control
- Demands a level of objectivity, fairness, and consistency from the appraiser that is often lacking and most certainly is not consistent throughout the organization
- Encourages mediocrity by rewarding those who manipulate or set safe goals
- Encourages employees to manipulate or "work the system"

- Develops cynicism and poor morale in a culture that becomes divided into winners and losers

Incentive Plans

The vast majority of corporations all over the world use some form of incentive plan to motivate all or some of their people to achieve performance. Yet in most cases, such incentives are divisive. To meet their goals, salespeople promise anything to close the sale—all of which later adds cost or trouble to the relationship with the customer. Senior managers make dangerous price reduction decisions when they are chasing a revenue incentive in the last quarter of the year.

In practice, much of what is called motivation in business is the alternate application of the stick and the carrot, punishment or incentive. As Frederick Herzberg has demonstrated in his writing, this push-me-pull-me management behavior may lead the individual to *move* (in that sense, incentives work), but it does not *motivate* them. Real motivation is to give individuals a reason to move; the individual acts because *he or she wants* to act. People motivated this way want to succeed for their own sake, but also for the sake of their manager, the organization, and perhaps most important the customer. But to achieve this level of response, the organization must drive out fear.

The Tentacles of Fear

Continued application of goal setting and other performance-related systems directed at individuals creates fear in the organization. Fear is the insidious cancer that prevents companies from operating to their maximum effectiveness over the long run. Fear is created by applying the traditional philosophies and behavior of management. Unfortunately, most managers just do not recognize that fear is present in their own operation. They would be horrified to believe that any of their own actions have contributed to a sense of fear among their subordinates.

Fear exists in the minds of managers and nonmanagement employees. Typical fears found in organizations are:

- *Reprisal*: fear of being disciplined or even terminated; fear of receiving poor appraisals or performance reviews
- *Failure*: fear of making a mistake or of making the wrong career move; fear of taking any risk
- *Providing information*: reluctance of managers and workers to volunteer information that they think may be used against them
- *Not knowing*: because information is power, fear on the part of managers that they do not know what is going on
- *Losing control*: selecting or promoting people who managers feel they can control
- *Change*: feeling more secure with what is known

Time Management

Sensible organization of time and selection of priorities is a commonsense approach to management. However, the mechanistic and overly detailed degree to which many managers use the concept has rendered it no better than a fad. The shelves at Office Depot—and sometimes office desks—appear inundated with the latest "organizers" or planning sheets. Time management practitioners seem to spend more time in managing time than they spend time in actually working.

Time management can be a negative tool in teamwork and general collaboration. There is a tendency for priority setting in the use of time to be an individualistic and totally selfish exercise. Individual priorities (like MBO individual objectives) can be a deterrent to teamwork if not developed in the context of group priorities. The selection of an individual's top six priorities, for example, can lead the person to concentrate working time on those six and ignore perhaps another twelve only-somewhat-less-important issues. Some of those twelve could be authorizations or vital information that others need to be able to accomplish their work.

My own personal practice, which I followed throughout corporate life, was simple but ran counter to some people's views of time management. My assistant or I would divide all my incoming mail, messages, etc. into three simple piles:

1. Important
2. Unimportant
3. For reading

The "for reading" pile was put into my briefcase for attention at home, probably in the bath. The "important" pile, too, is
then put aside, no matter how urgent the individual items. This
runs counter to the usual principles of time management. I then
give total attention to the "unimportant" pile. Experience shows
that this can be eliminated at great speed, leaving the day free
to concentrate on the important issues. The advantage of this
approach is that there is rarely a "pending" pile of unimportant
items that, through delay, became elevated to urgent or create
problems for other colleagues.

Long-Term Planning

Long-term planning is a beloved tool of large international corporations but one that is percolating down to their smaller brethren. As we shall see later, anticipatory management does demand
that the organization should look ahead; we spend some time
on it in Chapter 6. But that's a very different matter from the
operational plans prepared by the "business planning" department of many corporations. Few ever question the need for such
a department.

Their first step is to prepare "operational plans" in great
detail for the coming year. These are used to establish management goals and budgets for every country, division, or location.
This immediately elevates the exercise into the realm of company
politics, with some loss of objectivity. This is the base data for
MBO.

But the department is also told to prepare mid-term and
long-term business plans. Of course, some long-term "assumptions" are stated in terms of the technology and the marketplace
as guidelines for these inputs. The department's ability or resource to carry out meaningful research into these future areas is
limited, as so much of this planning is based on simplistic growth
factors or a wish list ritualistically applied to the current figures.
This exercise provides *accepted* forecasts for future development

of the business. Perhaps even more amazing (for the innocent), corporate executives happily spend hours listening to presentations on these "researched" projections. Of course, they exercise their egos, and to some extent their minds, to argue over relatively small digressions from the presented plan as though it were reality rather than a concoction. In many corporations, long-term planning can be likened to a religious festival in which all the participants dance to the ritual as if they believed in every facet of it. In business today, the reality is that three years is long-term.

Some of my scepticism for corporate management practices was sown in my early involvement in the process of corporate planning. I joined a major international computer corporation as market manager for the construction and medical markets. The latter part of my title was interesting in its own right. I knew nothing about the medical market for computers; the first I heard about that area was through my appointment letter with the expanded title. Naturally, an essential part of my role was to prepare marketing plans for the construction and medical markets. These were fundamentally short-term operational plans designed to instigate action, but they included some market projections as input to the long-term plan. I received praise for my plans, instigated and supported some actions, and for some reason was quickly promoted out of planning. At that stage, I was not senior enough to be given glimpse of the eventual corporate plan to which I had contributed. I spent a few years out in the tough operational fields of selling to Eastern Europe and then to the UK government. After some "years of achievement," I was promoted back to become the director for all the operations of which I was once a humble market manager. Now I was allowed to see the corporate plans; indeed, I was now responsible for producing them.

There is a tinge of nostalgia in admitting that my first week back in the corporate chateau was one of the most productive in my life. Close to my magnificent office and conference room was a substantial area dedicated to about thirty filing cabinets. After a couple of days, I realized that my key managers and research assistants were treating this area as some "ark of the covenant" or source of wisdom. I spent a long Saturday and Sunday of the intervening weekend supping at the wisdom in these filing cabinets. Stored deep in the heart of these records (in today's parlance, the marketing database) were my original marketing plans *and* their iteration into elements of the corporate long-term plans. In immense detail, they plotted the extraordinary success of products based on these nuggets of market wisdom. But these products no longer existed and the market conditions had totally changed! The five-year "long-term plans" were demonstrable nonsense. Yet managers had built and lost little empires on the basis of these sacred figures.

On the following Monday, I eliminated thirteen of the filing cabinets and questioned the need for a further six. It sent a shock through the system, but perhaps the most pertinent and amusing reaction was that of facilities management: "What are we going to do with all your redundant filing cabinets?" Hitherto, new managers had only ordered more, not sent them back! From my long experience, I would recommend that young managers rid themselves of filing cabinets or purge the planning database at the first opportunity.

A word to the wise. This is not a description of life in some failed corporate dinosaur of the past. This was Honeywell, a corporation for whom I have love and respect and whose fundamental values have since seen them through such nonsense.

Questions for the Reader

This chapter has looked at some management philosophies that have caused confusion in the past. The effect of these practices has lingered on and still pervades management behavior of today's corporations. The next chapter examines the impact of some more recent management revolutions and fads.

To end the chapter, the following questions may provide individual perspectives in considering the issues that have been raised. This is not an examination. You do not have to have a *correct* answer to every question. They are only designed to provoke you to ask more questions.

    1. In your own experience, have you seen managers accept objectives that in your opinion were unrealistic?

2. Have you ever compromised by accepting a goal that you considered ridiculous?
3. Have you ever been asked to accept goals that you considered ridiculous?
4. Have you ever experienced that desperate rush to complete performance appraisals on time?
5. Have you ever considered your own performance appraisal a charade that has to be endured?
6. Are all of your incentive goals relevant to your own area of control and responsibility?
7. Are all of your goals fair?
8. Do your managers organize their time to take account of *your* priorities?
9. Do you organize your time in relation to the goals or tasks you set your subordinates?
10. Do you feel that you can confidently predict what is going to happen in your own specific market or technology?

Chapter 4

Recent Revolutions

Since the late 1970s, the driving force for change has come from the so-called quality revolution and its many derivatives. Thousands of Western companies finally woke up to competition from Japan, and later the whole Pacific Basin, and launched some form of quality initiative. They met with mixed success. Evolutionary companies were not starting from scratch and were able to adapt many of the concepts to reinforce their existing quality culture. As we see later in this chapter, 3M and Marks and Spencer were good examples of this approach. Other companies used the concepts to become, and remain, world-class competitors. Unfortunately, the majority did not meet with the same measure of success.

In this chapter, we examine how these approaches were originally implemented and the reasons for their comparative failure. These experiences are pertinent to the whole theme of mindless change; they can be seen in the rise and fall of the "changeling children" of the quality revolution, namely:

- Corporate suggestion systems
- Quality circles
- Total quality management
- Empowerment
- Self-directed teams
- Business process reengineering
- Benchmarking
- ISO 9000
- Baldrige and other "business Oscars"
- Feng shui

Corporate Suggestion Systems

For a long time, Western companies believed that they were involving workers through the many variants of corporate suggestion systems. Executives were disappointed with the overall results, but to some extent this only served to reinforce their view that workers just didn't care. Their disappointment was founded on the relatively low number of suggestions and their perception of the quality or value of the content. A fairly typical example of the corporate system is provided by Prudential Assurance in the UK. In 1989, their seventeen thousand employees submitted 478 suggestions—of which 27 were later implemented. In fairness, the company has since revised their approach to releasing the potential of their employees and now receives hundreds of suggestions, of which a high proportion are implemented.

Despite a long history of comparative failure, corporate suggestion systems continue in many companies. Management is loath to accept that its efforts at employee involvement are at fault. The fundamental reason for the failure of these systems is that they usually call for *individual* suggestions and tend to evaluate proposals on the basis of how much money they save the company. Many corporations tried promotional programs such as "A buck a day" and other approaches that used humor and the "common touch" to enthuse the workers. These did succeed in raising the number of suggestions but again failed the management criteria. One such manager commented, "Well, the suggestions don't really amount to much—most of them are just about ways to make their job easier!" Naturally, as the workers saw that the majority of their contributions were being ignored, they soon lost interest. In any case, they had treated the process as an opportunity to repeat what they had been telling their supervisors for years about the silly way their work was organized.

This whole area of encouraging innovation is a good example of the evolutionary approach of Japanese companies. In the late 1950s, they became interested in Western "corporate suggestion systems" and experimented with similar approaches in Japan. Like their Western brethren, they were disappointed with the results and worked hard at finding the reason, including more visits to U.S. companies. They came to the conclusion that in their culture the individual worker did not want to stand out from the crowd in competing for personal success with a suggestion. They also noted that most Western suggestion systems focused on the financial value to the organization in evaluating contributions. As a result of their research, they changed the whole emphasis in employee involvement.

The Japanese encouraged small groups rather than the individual and the concept that a thousand small ideas were preferable to one big idea. The groups were the natural workgroups, and later cross-development voluntary groups with a wider perspective. This was the origin of the quality circle, which so intrigued the West in later years.

There was one other important change in emphasis introduced by the Japanese that accounted for their extraordinary success in employee involvement, and it also highlights a principle in evolutionary management philosophy. They implemented their approach in three distinct phases, each with its own emphasis on the real motivation of the employee.

1. Initially, the employees in their natural workgroups were encouraged to come up with ideas that would help them in their jobs and better the workplace environment. In other words, *start* with the issues that hassle the employee—the selfsame issue that earned the contempt of Western managers.

Totally new markets create their own ambience, which goes beyond the intrinsic value of the new products. For example, introduction of the first computers bestowed the cachet of "technology leader" on initial customers. "They must be special; they have a computer." In the concept-based service market, the ambience is more subtle, involving a relationship between the provider and the purchaser. The customer is seen as having made a declared act of faith in both the product and the supplier (or guru). Such an environment encourages a religious fervor in which many of the brethren become zealots blind to any doubt. This is exactly what happened in the quality movement. Crosby, Deming, and, to a lesser extent, Juran were previously respected as thought-provoking authors or academics, but now they became gurus, each surrounded with their band of faithful adherents.

And then the myths began.

Gurus are soon surrounded by cohorts who turn each of their half-considered thoughts into *ex cathedra* statements that must be deemed infallible. I was one such early acolyte, and I well remember issues resolved by "quoting from page 187," etc., similarly to the way religious issues are always answered by biblical quotations. At the same time, the guru of choice must be extolled in competition with the others. This is how the myths are propagated: the myth that it was Crosby who invented zero defects, and the myth that Deming changed Japan. One can never be sure, but one reasonably suspects that the gurus themselves also came to believe the myths. From the perspective of business as a whole, the decade of the quality guru was initially invigorating, but later it became suffocating.

The myth of zero defects is of no consequence, but in any case Crosby did become its principal exponent. The myth about Deming and Japan does matter and is pertinent to the central theme of this book. The abiding danger of the Deming myth is that it gave legitimacy to the need for revolutionary change as the answer to the competitive challenge from the East. But the myth was based on a false premise: *there never was a Japanese revolution.*

The Deming myth began when NBC-TV produced a documentary in June 1980 entitled "If Japan Can, Why Can't We?" NBC gave credit for the "economic miracle" in Japan to Dr.

Deming and christened him "the father of the Japanese revolution." This was palpable nonsense. In retrospect, it is difficult to
escape the conclusion that the wounded pride of the United
States was somehow ameliorated by the belief that the inventor
of this new phase was an American. From then on, Deming became a prophet in his own land and was described by another
U.S. business leader, William E. Conway, as the "father of the
third wave of the industrial revolution." Now Deming has become the father of *two* revolutions!

Deming certainly had an influence on the Japanese, starting
when the Union of Japanese Scientists and Engineers (JUSE) invited him to address them in June 1950. For Deming adherents,
this event has been elevated to a status close to that of the Ser-
mon on the Mount. This was followed by a meeting with the
presidents of twenty-one major Japanese companies, including
present-day world giants Sony, Mitsubishi, Nissan, and Toyota.
But others, including Juran, had a similar—some consider it a
greater—influence. Both Deming and Juran are recognized in
Japan for their contribution to the development of management
thinking. The Deming Prize for Quality is still eagerly sought by
Japanese companies, and Juran's contribution is recognized by
the prestigious Order of the Sacred Treasure awarded to him in
1981 by Emperor Hirohito.

In considering the early postwar influence on Japan, it
would be foolish to ignore the incredible achievements of America's first and last proconsul, Gen. Douglas MacArthur. Under his
leadership the TWI (Training Within Industries) agency contributed greatly to awakening Japanese interest in the management
practices of the West. TWI introduced Japanese management to
Deming, Juran, and many others. But to believe that the Japanese jumped on the bandwagon of a specific guru is to wholly
misunderstand Japanese culture. It also exhibits a total lack of
comprehension of the concept of evolutionary management.

The cataclysmic defeat of 1945 certainly opened Japan to
external influences, but it viewed opportunities for commercial
success holistically. The Japanese listened assiduously to Western experts but continued to travel the world to quietly learn
and decide what practices and techniques could be *adapted* to
fit Japanese culture. This evolutionary and traditional approach,
used by business for centuries, has now been reinvented by Rob-

ert Camp and is called benchmarking. The Japanese use of the concept was so successful that they developed a whole new approach to management and to releasing the potential of workers. This was the real basis for TQM.

The theme of mindless change is well demonstrated by the contrasting experience of the phases of the TQM movement in the West. The initial phase in the late 1970s spawned the pioneers. These companies had to give long and serious thought as to how to apply these new concepts to their own business culture. They didn't have the advantage—or as history now teaches us, the disadvantage—of the specific prescribed solutions of the gurus. This phase forged dedicated leaders who made quality a way of life in their organizations. They truly understood the Japanese experience. A significant proportion of those pioneers, companies such as 3M, Procter and Gamble, and Marks and Spencer, are still recognized as leaders in continuous and evolutionary improvement. Intriguingly, the process followed by the pioneers actually took the same evolutionary route as the Japanese did in developing their own approach to TQM. Rather than sitting at the feet of an American guru and then instantly changing, the Japanese took their time studying the West and the ideas of the leaders of American industry. In those days, the United States was the world-acknowledged master of technology and management practices. The Japanese made visit after visit until they really understood what was happening. They returned home, thought carefully about what they had learned, and gradually developed answers that fit their own culture. Rather than imposing an alien solution with mindless abandon on their distinct culture, they harnessed the best of the West in tandem with the best of their own traditions.

Then TQM moved into the phase of the followers, which gathered pace in the eighties. The mad rush onto the TQM bandwagon included thousands of small and medium companies, but it also included giant corporations such as General Motors, ICI (Imperial Chemical Industries), and British Petroleum, which spent millions of dollars on the concept of quality management. Eager to emulate the pioneers and catch up, the followers accepted simple absolutes almost without question and were delighted to find that now there were gurus able to offer them how-to methods of education and implementation. The followers did not have to "think out" issues for themselves. The so-called proven methods of Crosby and others were there, presented to them on a plate. These methods cost a lot of money, but that was preferable to indecision and delay. Only now has growing awareness of the ultimate failure of these initiatives among the followers bred scepticism about TQM.

In retrospect, TQM has been a comparative failure. Some companies did use the concepts as change agents to redress the problems caused by the unthinking short-term management of the 1950s and 1960s. In fairness, most companies did improve because improvement was in focus; but few were able to realize the full potential that the TQM concepts provided, namely, the opportunity to get back on track and close the competitive gap with the Pacific rim. This comparative disappointment with what was being achieved with TQM was to lead directly to an even more radical concept, which became known as business process reengineering.

Looking back, one can see a distinct difference between the way evolutionary companies and revolutionary companies used the TQM concepts. To evolutionary companies, the concepts were not totally new; they had been practicing many of the elements for years. They used the general focus on quality as an agent to *reinforce* their improvement culture and to ensure that these concepts were a natural part of the "woodwork." The revolutionary organizations were so besotted by quality, as then proclaimed, that they established a whole new edifice within their companies in its honor. Hundreds of quality improvement teams, steering committees, and quality councils ensured that quality became a separate exercise rather than the normal pattern of work. Like all revolutions in history, the practice destroyed the concepts upon which it was instigated.

The point can be illustrated by comparing the approach to TQM taken by 3M and General Motors. 3M, an evolutionary company, certainly listened to the quality gurus. Senior managers attended the Crosby Quality College, and others spent time with both Deming and Juran. Steadily, 3M developed its own approach for use in all its operations in the United States and abroad. Eventually, the company formed its own Quality Institute to teach the approach to suppliers and other interested companies. Before it started, 3M was already a "quality company," but it used the TQM process to reinforce a focus on continuous improvement.

General Motors also wanted to do things its way, up to a point. They were more concerned with a quick fix of how to teach their managers the new concepts rather than adapt the concepts themselves. Instead of sending hundreds of managers to Crosby's Quality College in Florida, they sent about thirty managers for six months to the same college to go through the same training that Crosby gave to all his instructor-consultants. This cost them close to $100,000 for each individual trained. Of course, they believed that they were learning how to implement the prescribed Crosby approach to quality management. What they actually learned was how to *project* the process rather than put it into practice, which was exactly what the Crosby staff were taught. GM did get better, but for all the money they threw at the issue they should have been disappointed. The fundamental GM culture was not substantially modified.

There is one major lesson to learn from the TQM experience: Mindlessly following a guru is a recipe for disaster. Gurus, consultants, and practitioners can never be more than facilitators to assist organizations to *think* and then develop approaches that best fit the organizational culture. No organization should launch any companywide initiative without first making a thorough assessment of the need to change, its relative position, and the cultural barriers to achievement. The need for all companies to be involved in continuous improvement is as strong as ever, but individual organizations must own their own process.

In reality, the concepts of the quality gurus were neither revolutionary nor even particularly new. They represent a return to common sense in the management of business. The real contribution of the gurus has been to refocus the eyes of management and light up areas that had become hidden by previous periods of mindless management. They were helped by the fact that the Japanese were devastating American markets. The executive threshold of pain had been broached.

Empowerment

Great damage is being done by overuse and misuse of the term *empowerment*. We are reaching a stage where the word means whatever a particular manager wants it to mean. Some of the examples often quoted to show the importance of empowerment are laughable. To allow the counter hand at a burger bar to distribute additional sachets of sauce if the customer wants them is not empowerment, it's a modification to the standard. If the same counter hand were allowed to close down the burger bar for an hour because she believed that the french fries were below standard, *that* would be empowerment. In some cultures, management's use of the words "employee empowerment" can be a harbinger of fear. The employees' expectation is that they are going to have to take the responsibility for everything that goes wrong.

Empowerment quite simply means granting supervisors or workers permission to give the customer priority over other issues in the operation. In practical terms, it relates to the resources, skill, time, and support to become leaders rather than controllers or mindless robots. The concept lies at the heart of managing with common sense and is developed in Chapter 12.

Self-Directed Teams

In recent years, the subject of self-directed teams has become an industry in its own right. Hundreds of books, videos, and cassettes on varying aspects of teamwork dominate business bookshops and libraries. At the same time, a host of consultants (who like to think of themselves as behavioral scientists) and training organizations make a healthy living from the concept of teamwork. This new emphasis on teams has been described as the essential element in the "managerial revolution."

As with all revolutions, there is actually nothing new about teams in the business environment. Prior to the move toward specialization and division, which was described earlier, the self-directed team was the natural way to organize work. It still is in the smaller firm, and in particular the family business. In essence, Taylor and scientific management ushered in big business, which in time exaggerated the divisions and bureaucracy that stifle teamwork. Steadily, large mainframe computers allowed already big corporations to become colossal; by the 1960s the idea of teams was almost extinct. The team was essentially a small-company concept. But the evolution of computing and other technologies was changing the nature of work. "Unthinking" jobs were being eliminated and "knowledge" workers were growing in significance. Attending to people and their behavior was now back in fashion, and business rediscovered the team.

Interest in Japanese managerial methods and the concentration on quality management in the eighties increased emphasis on introducing teamwork. Now the whole team movement exhibits some of the characteristics of the TQM revolution. Everybody is for teamwork, nobody is against it, and yet in truth actual practice has been very disappointing. It would seem that the success or comparative failure of self-directed teams lies in the motivation for their introduction. Once again, the difference in approach between the evolutionary companies who adapt and the others who adopt is apparent.

Evolutionary companies always valued their people, as indicated by their high investment in education and training. Teamwork was fostered in those companies some decades before the concept became fashionable. To my knowledge, management development and training in 3M, Procter and Gamble, Honeywell, Marks and Spencer, and Toyota included comprehension of the theories of Elton Mayo, Abraham Maslow and the hierarchy of needs, and Douglas McGregor with Theories X and Y. All of these lie at the heart of team dynamics. Just as with TQM, evolutionary companies used the emphasis on teams as supportive or as a reenforcement to their existing value systems. They can usually provide examples of the power of self-directed teams. In essence, they are committed to the team ethos as part of their strategy of thinking small and keeping focused on continuous movement.

Quick-fix revolutionary companies tend to view technology and the concept of self-directed teams with an entirely different motivation. They are usually both seen as providing the opportunity to get rid of people and to reduce costs. Using technology to redesign processes and to enable creation of self-directed teams is the principal element in reengineering and downsizing. Revolutionary companies generally succeeded in their short-term objectives, but the concept of using teamwork over an extended period failed and the long-term success of those companies was put in peril. In one sense, this is an obvious conclusion that should have been clear from the outset. In that environment, asking people to work together in teams for the greater good of the company is a little like asking turkeys to vote for Thanksgiving and Christmas.

Self-directed teams succeed if the environment or organizational value systems are conducive to success; if not, they fail. The reasons identified by a number of writers for why teams don't work have a direct relationship to the values of evolutionary companies described in the third part of this book, "Common Sense." Lack of vision, confused objectives, personality conflicts, weak leadership, and lack of team trust are direct opposites to—or more accurately the result of the lack of—the evolutionary values and a clear focus on customers and processes. A mindless approach to implementing a team-based culture will fail.

Business Process Reengineering

Business process reengineering (BPR) has followed TQM as the fashionable management quick-fix route to performance improvement. BPR also has its own gurus, led by Michael Hammer, author of *Reengineering the Corporation: A Manifesto for Business Revolution* (yet another guru with a new guillotine). He defined BPR as a "fundamental rethink and radical redesign of business processes to achieve dramatic improvements in critical contemporary measures of performance, such as cost, quality, service, and speed."*

The approach is based on the premise that continuous incremental improvement (the perceived objective of TQM) is not capable of meeting the challenge of the global marketplace. To succeed, companies need major breakthroughs in performance to leapfrog the competition. BPR aims for dramatic improvements, not small steps to achieve slow and steady progress. Rather than 10 percent improvements, BPR expects to cut product development cycles by 50 percent, to cut order delivery times from one month to one day, and to take 60–80 percent out of costs while at the same time improving service levels. Figure 4-1

*New York: HarperCollins, 1993.

illustrates this idealistic view of BPR. Claiming such a level of dramatic change is likely to catch the attention of most executives. However, before jumping on the BPR bandwagon, they would be wise to pause for thought.

Following my own book on the subject, I was asked by an executive whether I could help his corporation achieve similar breakthroughs. He looked surprised at my reply: "That depends on how badly you have been running the company over the last few years." Of course, most companies gain from questioning the performance of their current practices and processes, but this does not mean that all will find the same opportunities for dramatic breakthrough. In Figure 4-1, the dream route to excellence is illustrated as A to D, but counting on incorporating the dramatic upturn from B to C is far from reality. This portrays the BPR sales pitch, but it is not what really happens.

Turn now to Figure 4-2, and we have a clear comparison between the performance of our evolutionary companies and the real position of the so-called breakthrough revolutionary companies. Each element in the illustrated journey in both figures, that is, A to B, B to C, and C to D, has lessons and examples for the unwary.

Let's start at the beginning with A to B, typical of the corporate leaders in BPR. (You find one of their representatives making a presentation at most major BPR conferences; it might be Xerox, Texas Instruments, AT&T, and IBM.) None of these corporations were quietly climbing through the gentle uplands of incremental improvement depicted in Figure 4-1. They were in actuality coming out of a period of dangerous free fall (Figure 4-2, section A to B) caused by their own complacency, incompetence, disastrous management strategies, and—in the case of AT&T—the additional problem of aggressive external legislation. In other words, their existing management practices were fundamentally flawed and were in urgent need of overhaul. Each had failed to anticipate changes in areas key to their business such as customer perceptions, product technologies, and political awareness.

There are many opportunities for dramatic breakthroughs in business performance that lie outside the area of BPR. Totally new products or the emergence of totally new markets, as for example invention of the VCR or the opening of Eastern Europe

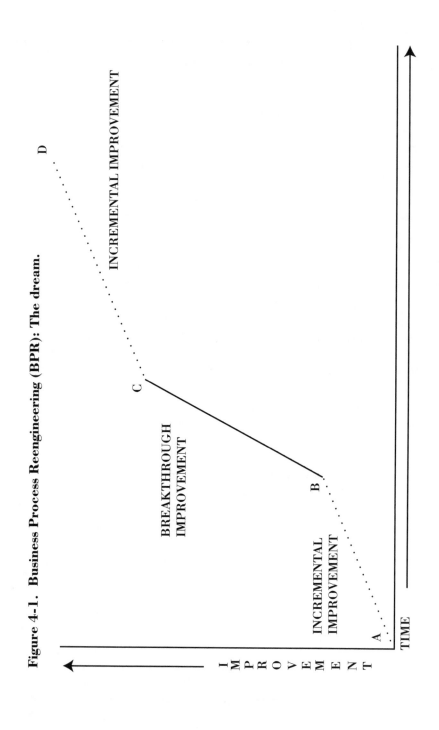

Figure 4-1. Business Process Reengineering (BPR): The dream.

Figure 4-2. BPR: The Reality.

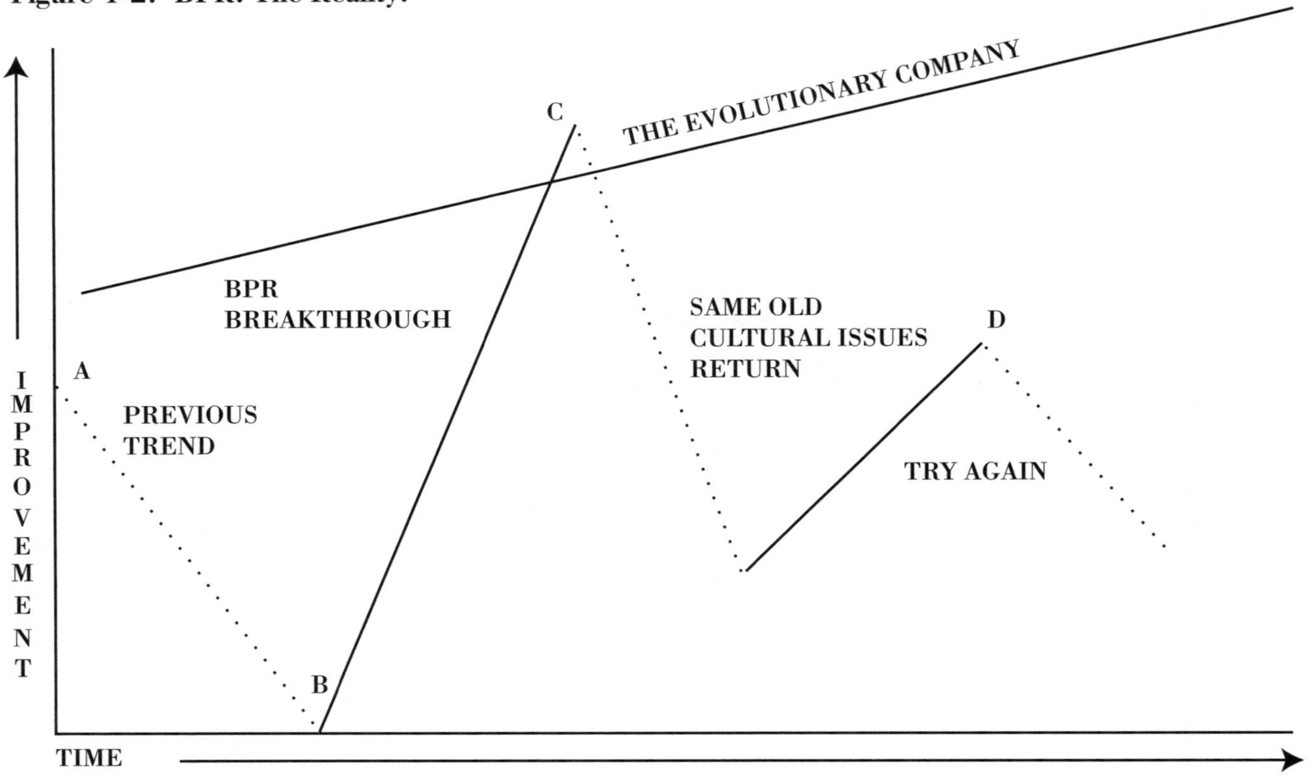

and Russia, are cases in point, though no doubt both would be aided by more efficient business processes. BPR, on the other hand, concerns itself with reengineering or redesigning company business processes and management practices. The opportunities for dramatic breakthrough are usually concealed in these arenas:

- Continuous mindless management has created an accretion of redundant procedures and processes.
- Fearful employees and middle management have erected a series of defensive walls that inhibit communication, hide the facts, and screw the customer.
- Converging technologies provide opportunities to work in a different way.

A moment's thought leads to the conclusion that a badly managed company has the most to gain from BPR. This is also why the evolutionary companies that are continuously redesigning their processes are not attracted to *radical* change. Paradoxically, adherents of BPR are least likely to maintain their breakthrough improvement, which failure is indicated in the C to D part of Figure 4-2.

Companies that embark on the BPR route as a "bold" and revolutionary move to recover from previous mindless management of their processes exhibit two tendencies in implementation and maintenance of the breakthrough:

1. They fail to modify their operating culture and therefore fall back into their old destructive ways and quickly dissipate any advantage gained from redesign. The same old cultural issues and barriers return, and they are soon almost back to where they started (part C to D of Figure 4-2). This has also created a climate in which it is much more difficult to mount another revolution.

2. As born-again converts to the new religion, they approach BPR as zealots. Their ruthless mapping and reengineering of business processes uses every facet of new technology and management theory to simplify processes and *eliminate* people. A mechanistic approach ignores or is unaware of all the proven issues of natural variation and the usefulness of experience. Additionally, this approach pays little attention to the organization's

value systems as a reference point for evaluating change. BPR has often resulted in the very worst aspects of downsizing. As a result, there are few knowledgeable heads left to help modify the excesses of the new design and maintain incremental improvement.

My own advice, based on the bitter experience of companies involved in BPR, is to practice a simple rule. If a redesigned process calls for eliminating ten people, argue first for the release of only six, and in the end never settle for termination of more than eight. The very act of simplifying the process establishes new relationships with other processes and variable customers. Despite all the tools of simulation and pilot proving, I have yet to meet a reengineered business process that envisaged every contingency. If the organization has cut too far, there is no one left who has actually been involved in the task and has knowledge of how to get the process out of the pit.

Perhaps a saving grace of the present enthusiasm for BPR is that the majority of organizations that use the term are not really engaged in the radical transformation urged upon them by the gurus. The risks involved are such that their cultures would not survive the shock. In reality, they are engaged in process redesign. For most companies, this still represents radical change. Figure 4-3 illustrates the essential differences between process improvement (TQM), process redesign, and process reengineering.

Relationship Between Improvement, Redesign, and Reengineering

In practice, process redesign is a natural evolution of TQM. James Harrington, a minor guru of that period, described the concepts of BPR long before Hammer wrote his book. But there is nothing very new in any of the business fashions. In 1958, Harry P. Cemach and F. W. Lowe (a former general manager of Harrods, the famed London store) wrote a book with the prosaic title *Work Study in the Office*. It describes the same process and uses exactly the same symbols as are now used for BPR process

Figure 4-3. Relationship between process improvement, process redesign, and process reengineering.

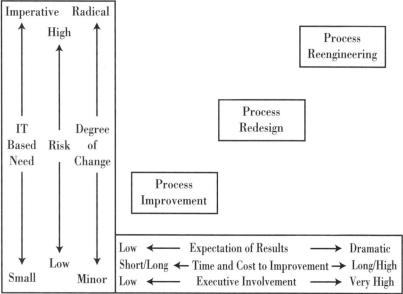

mapping. It differs from the current approach in its degree of focus on the opportunities available from converging technologies. In other words, once again we have evidence that our evolutionary companies did not need to wait for a guru-led revolution; they were practicing process redesign thirty years ago. They were using the commonsense tool of questioning work patterns, and they used the same language of systems to describe work activities as we do today. Nothing much really changes.

As an old warhorse, I note nostalgically that I used the techniques learned in the 1950s to reengineer the processes of electioneering over the period of the 1964 and 1966 general elections in the UK. The trend at the time was running against my own political allegiance, but each of those campaigns achieved a swing well against the trend. Indeed, the second effort was described by a political pundit as "a chromium-plated campaign." The processes of electioneering were dramatically improved, but not quite enough. A wiser electorate was still able to reject me. But the approach has remained with me forever, and it still boils down to:

- What are we doing?
- Why are we doing it?
- Do we need to go on doing it?
- If so, how are we doing it?
- Is there another way to do it?
- (Followed by) when, where, and who?

Downsizing

Downsizing is a discomfiting word, which is probably why some executives prefer to use the neutral (though distinctly euphemistic) word *rightsizing*. It is a cantankerous child of the BPR movement, but it differs in the sense that the initial motivation to act is different. Downsizing is driven by the god of short-term profitability rather than that of process improvement. Its primary focus is on maximum elimination of people rather than long-term delight of customers. The quick-fix executive has seized upon downsizing as an early opportunity to impress Wall Street analysts with his or her objective management of the corporation.

Research into the impact of downsizing has unearthed an interesting factor in comparing revolutionary and evolutionary companies. In almost every case, major examples of downsizing have occurred following a change of chief executive; these new executives were often appointed from outside the company. That a fresh new wind blows away the cobwebs is another revolutionary fallacy. These new executives are desperately seeking a way to make a big bang. In contrast, evolutionary companies, almost without exception, appoint their top executives from within the culture and values of the corporation. We return to this intriguing difference in Part Three of this book.

The experience of downsizing has clearly changed the environment in employee relations. The best modern managers are attempting to implement participative management styles and value systems designed to encourage meaningful open and frank communication throughout their organizations. Yet at the same time, frequently quoted examples of downsizing are influencing the workforce. The image of downsizing as a natural recourse for executives is destroying trust and loyalty and is bringing back adversarial relationships at all levels of business. A recent U.S. national survey quoted in the *Chicago Tribune* reported that 35 percent of middle managers distrust their immediate supervisor and that 55 percent of all employees do not believe anything that top management says. In an environment where highly skilled managers and knowledge workers (once considered prize employees) are looking over their shoulders with fear, what chance is there for trust in the corporation?

Now even the gurus of downsizing are retreating and admitting that they were wrong. Stephen Roach, chief economist at Morgan Stanley, one of America's biggest investment banks, was a strong proponent of downsizing but has since had second thoughts. Roach has been quoted in the press as saying that downsizing was fine if companies were making genuine improvements in performance. However, the evidence is that "slash and burn" has become a strategy in itself. Roach continues, "If productivity gains were truly being made, they would have been accompanied by increases in worker compensation."

Since 1979, employment in manufacturing in Britain has fallen from seven million to below four million. This has been represented as a productivity miracle because output per head has risen by 80 percent. Overall output, however, has risen by less than 8 percent. The view that downsizing is the source of productivity growth is not substantiated. Indeed, companies that turned in the best productivity performance were just as likely to be those that hired more workers. To quote a British journalist, Keith Waterhouse, commenting in the *London Daily Mail* on such a report, "it would seem that the best way to sell sprockets is not to fire the sales manager but to go out there and sell sprockets. Amazing."

It is now clear that the short-term economic benefits of downsizing are questionable, but we are also beginning to realize that the long-term effects on business and society are positively damaging. How many loyal and able employees have been sacrificed in this latest example of mindless management?

In the context of this book, once again there is a simple lesson to be learned for management of the future. The need for substantial downsizing, as for example at IBM or General Motors, is more often the result of previous bad management. Lead-

bids. This has led to a cynical boardroom joke: at a celebratory party for accreditation, the CEO turns to a colleague and says, "OK, so that's quality dealt with; now we can get back to running the business." There is some truth behind the joke because this attitude does exist. But it is not the whole truth, and it actually casts an interesting light on the whole era of quality-related revolutions.

During the research for a book entitled *Does TQM Really Work?* published in 1993, I was very surprised to find that the estimated failure rate for TQM was more than twice as high for the United States as for the UK. I was not chauvinistic enough to believe that this was wholly due to the competence of UK managers vis-à-vis their U.S. counterparts. But the research had also led to some other facts, and the possible correlation was intriguing. At that time, fewer than two thousand U.S. companies had ISO 9000 accreditation, while the corresponding figure for the United Kingdom exceeded twenty-five thousand. When one considers the relative size of the two economies, the figures are even more extraordinary. A little history is needed to explain this discrepancy.

ISO 9000 is derived from the British standard BS5750, which in turn was derived from quality standards on which the U.S. Department of Defense and the British Ministry of Defense agreed for delivery of military equipment to NATO and to each other. Under Thatcher's drive to revitalize Britain, the UK Department of Trade and Industry decided to make accreditation to BS5750 a major element in their "national quality campaign." The breadth of the campaign and the assistance to smaller companies were wider than the introduction of standards alone; this was indicated by the advertising launch slogan, "Quality is too important to leave to your quality manager." The success of this campaign, together with the curbing of archaic trade union power, probably accounts for a major proportion of the massive investment in Britain from Japan, Korea, and the United States. It is not an accident that the erstwhile spent, tired, and old-fashioned UK at the time of this writing now leads Germany, France, and the rest of Europe in all the parameters of economic success.

Of course, Great Britain has the same incidence of companies that exhibit the attitudes of the boardroom joke. But in both the United Kingdom and the United States, there are many companies that would approach TQM or other passing initiatives in a similar manner. The lesson to be learned is that a period of disciplined thinking at many levels in the organization eventually pays dividends. The exercise of understanding and seeking accreditation to ISO 9000 would appear to be an educational influence in development of a thinking evolutionary company (well, at least in the area of quality).

ISO 9000 may be a latter-day quality saint in the United States, but its gathering pace may do more in the long run to change the mass of U.S. companies in the field of quality than all the gurus combined.

Baldrige and the Business Oscars

The whole concept of individual company awards for quality or any other aspect of business performance is suspect. The Baldrige, the Deming, and the European Foundation for Quality Management (EFQM) Awards tend to focus on and legitimize a particular "fashionable" approach to business management. A reexamination of the companies featured in Tom Peters and Robert Waterman's famous book *In Search of Excellence* and some early award winners helps make the point. Few of those original companies would now earn the "excellent" badge.

At the very best, the assessment processes on which the awards are based can only be a snapshot appraisal of a company's performance. Identifying core competencies and taking measurements *over a period of years* against the award criteria form little or no part of the award assessment. Yet these are the real arbiters of long-term success. These assessments suffer from some of the dangerous influences noted in the discussion about personnel appraisal in Chapter 3. It is also true that the principal motivation for corporations to aspire to these awards is for marketing purposes, similarly to seeking ISO 9000 accreditation.

Success in such awards and the continuing media attention they bring can breed complacency and overconfidence to management of the featured companies. The performance of IBM demonstrates this aspect to the full. Throughout the 1980s, IBM was extolled as the epitome of quality and one of Peters and Waterman's excellent companies; in other words, the leader for us all to imitate. Yet we all now know (Compaq and others had anticipated and knew it at the time) that IBM's business strategy during that period was hopelessly wrong. Whatever their quality, they managed their core marketing competency with incompetence. As we have said before, it cost thousands of loyal employees their jobs. Company awards are not much solace to people standing in line at job centers.

For many organizations, the resources expended in chasing these awards are immense and would be better used in ensuring continued success rather than transient awards. Typically, though, teams of the "best" people are assembled from across the corporation to develop the "presentation" for consideration by the assessors. The team gains some valuable experience but is usually dissipated following the exercise. There can only be a few winners, and so great companies that should know better appear to be happy that they rated a "visit" by the assessors. It has become a new form of Pavlovian dance to satisfy the egos of executives.

If these awards have any value, it is that quality is brought into focus as an essential element in business success. That may be of more help to the thousands of little companies that are influenced to improve rather than those directly involved in the award process.

Feng Shui

It is very difficult to take this latest management fad at all seriously, though some major corporations seem convinced. Feng Shui is claimed to be an ancient Chinese philosophy based on the positive focus of life forces. It is claimed to make work bearable and has been described as the caring philosophy for business life in the nineties. Feng Shui teaches that the world's natural forces invisibly surround every individual and every building, not unlike the Judeo-Christian belief that God is everywhere. Believers claim that this force can be controlled in the business environment to create energy and peace.

As a skeptic, I see it all as further evidence of mindless change. I have not been convinced that any of the following dramatically improve business performance:

- Putting fish tanks full of carp in your office
- Never wearing yellow clothes
- Ensuring that all plants in the office have rounded leaves

Buzzwords

The development of technology has impacted the language of business. Some of these changes have been evolutionary and naturally added to the lexicon available for purposeful communication at work. However, technology has also spawned a new type of jargon that is nearly as incomprehensible as it appears sophisticated. Many managers seem drawn to this growing fad and must include a buzzword or buzzphrase in all their communications.

This trend has been growing over several decades. As long ago as the 1960s, the computer division of Honeywell produced an amusing marketing game for their prospects and customers that recognized the new fad. Called the "Buzzphrase, Buzzword Generator," it purported to help equip the reader for technical writing. Their writing system was based on their devised "Simplified Integrated Modular Prose (SIMP) writing system" and allowed the user to create thousands of incomprehensible but intelligent-sounding terms. You may enjoy a short interlude by experimenting with this Honeywell tool and producing some of your own phrases and sentences from the examples in Figure 4-4.

Conclusion

This chapter has looked at a number of current management philosophies and fashions that, when misused, have caused confusion at work. The future doesn't require that all these current management practices should be instantly rejected. That would in itself be mindless and create a dangerous void. But all organizations do have to evaluate what needs to be preserved and what is hindering successful evolution of the business.

Questions for the Reader

1. Have you experienced frustration at management indifference to your suggestions or to the views of a team of which you are a part, about problems you are meeting?
2. Have you been involved in some form of quality initiative that failed to live up to expectations?
3. Have you received education, training, or awareness sessions in techniques and approaches that appeared to have little relevance to your actual problems?
4. Have you experienced redesign and upheaval in the way you work that in the end made little difference?
5. Are you aware of fear or insecurity in your job as a result of management action or pronouncement?
6. Have you been involved in preparing data for outside bodies knowing the facts to be at best dubious?
7. From what you have read so far, would you evaluate your company as an evolutionary or revolutionary organization?

Figure 4-4. Honeywell's 1960s "Buzzphrase, Buzzword Generator."

Buzzphrase, Buzzword Generator

BUZZPHRASE	
SIMP TABLE A	*SIMP TABLE B*
1. In particular,	1. a large portion of the interface coordination communication
2. On the other hand,	2. a constant flow of effective information
3. However,	3. the characterization of specific criteria
4. Similarly,	4. initiation of critical subsystem development
5. As a resultant implication,	5. the fully integrated test program
6. In this regard,	6. the product configuration baseline
7. Based on integral subsystem considerations,	7. any associated supporting element
8. For example,	8. the incorporation of additional mission constraints
9. Thus,	9. the independent functional principle
10. In respect to specific goals,	10. a primary interrelationship between system and/or subsystem technologies

If you have had the nagging feeling lately that your virtuosity at the game of terminology ping-pong has somewhat plateaued, rest easy. Technology has created a new type of jargon that is nearly as incomprehensible as it is sophisticated.

This technical writing kit is based on the Simplified Integrated Modular Prose (SIMP) writing system. Using this kit, anyone who can count to 10 can write up to 40,000 discrete, well-balanced grammatically correct sentences using the buzzphrase section or the same number of incomprehensible intelligent sounding technical terms with the buzzword generator.

To put SIMP to work, arrange the modules in A-B-C-D order. Take any four-digit number, 8751 for example, and read Phrase 8 off Module A, Phrase 7 off Module B, etc. The result is a SIMP sentence.

BUZZWORD		
COLUMN 1	COLUMN 2	COLUMN 3
1. integrated	1. management	1. options
2. total	2. organizational	2. flexibility
3. systematized	3. monitored	3. capability
4. parallel	4. reciprocal	4. mobility
5. functional	5. digital	5. programming
6. responsive	6. logic	6. concept
7. optical	7. transitional	7. timephase
8. synchronized	8. incremental	8. projection
9. compatible	9. third-generation	9. hardware
10. balanced	10. policy	10. contingency

BUZZPHRASE	
SIMP TABLE C	SIMP TABLE D
1. must utilize and be functionally interwoven with	1. the sophisticated hardware.
2. maximizes the probability of project success and minimizes the cost and time required for	2. the anticipated fourth generation equipment.
3. adds explicit performance limits to	3. the subsystem compatibility testing.
4. necessitates that urgent consideration be applied to	4. the structural design, based on system engineering concepts.
5. requires considerable systems analysis and trade-off studies to arrive at	5. the preliminary qualification limit.
6. is further compounded, when taking into account	6. the evolution of specifications over a given time period.
7. presents extremely interesting challenges to	7. the philosophy of commonality and standardization.
8. recognizes the importance of other systems and the necessity for	8. the greater fight-worthiness concept.
9. effects a significant implementation of	9. any discrete configuration mode.
10. adds overriding performance constraints to	10. the total system rationale.

Add a few more four-digit numbers to make a SIMP paragraph.

After you have mastered the basic technique, you can realize the full potential of SIMP by arranging the modules in D-A-C-B order, B-A-C-D order or A-D-C-B order. In these advanced configurations, some additional commas may be required.

For those who require that snap word the buzzword may be utilized. Merely select a digit from each of the three columns and combine the words opposite each number into your own technical jargon. For example, select 4, 0, and 1 and you generate "parallel policy options," an expression bound to command instant respect—and confusion!

Chapter 5

Mindless Education

By education most have been misled; So they believe, because they were so bred.

John Dryden (1631–1700)

The discipline of colleges and universities is in general contrived, not for the benefit of students, but for the interest, or more properly speaking, for the ease of the masters.

Samuel Smiles (1812–1904)

Aye, 'tis well enough for a servant to be bred at an University—But the education is a little too pedantic for a gentleman.

William Congreve (1670–1729)

Education and training clearly play a major part in the development of business managers. So in looking at the performance of managers across the corporate business world, it is necessary to consider how they were developed. This is a very broad subject capable of sustaining many books in its own right. For the purposes of this book, education and training is confined to some general comments in the following areas:

- The state of education
- Faculty and students
- Learning from history
- Business schools
- Corporate education and training
- Consultants and gurus

The State of Education

Mindless changes have been perpetrated by mindless managers. The majority of these managers have not been recruited from a host of natural oafs or village idiots. For the most part, they are university graduates, and in a large number of cases they attended the *best* business schools. There are two sides to the educational coin, though, because we have also identified other managers (presumably from the same sources) who do not exhibit the same propensity for mindless change. This chapter aims to identify those factors that differ in education and company induction to help us answer two questions: (1) How do so many managers learn to be mindless? (2) How do a few managers learn that they always have time to think?

These questions are pertinent to the debate about the efficacy of Western educational systems to meet the future needs of society and business. There is little argument about the fundamental need to increase and improve the education and training of a greater proportion of nationwide populations. The debate is generally centered around how increased education is to be funded and the specific ways to achieve standards. Even this debate is becoming confused. The perceived need to provide *every* student with "self-esteem" requires that everyone can make the standard. The latest educational concentration on "attitude" is reducing rather than heightening standards. There are two paradoxes buried in those arguments that are mirrored in the management practices of business. Both paradoxes are rooted in the continuous competition between quantity and quality. Some would argue that the compromises have reached the stage where society is losing out on both fronts.

The first paradox stems from the sheer scale of the issue. In many countries, the combined population of students and faculty and the services involved in major universities have created campuses that rival substantial towns in their size. These massive institutions have steadily developed introverted cultures that have moved them away from their original purpose. The management and senior faculty of some universities exhibit the chateau-management tendencies of business corporations. They have increasingly adopted the same techniques as those corporations in attempting to meet their own mass-production requirements. Revenue rather than customer focus, short-term financial budgeting, departmentalized and hierarchical organizations, and overspecialized curricula are just some examples. Modern universities are hectic hives of mindless activity rather than quiet havens for thought. The paradox is that in chasing the laudable objective of educating the masses, "centers of learning" have sacrificed their traditional values. Under the unrelenting pressure of numbers and the bureaucratic obsession with grades, our universities and business schools are in danger of confusing the difference between education and training. Vast numbers of graduating students have been taught *what* to think, rather than *how* to think.

The second paradox is similar but relates to the amount of information and knowledge available to the student. Information technology provides easy access to accumulated knowledge on a vastly increasing scale. The action-oriented values of our society lead the student to believe that knowledge must be learned rather than understood. There is little time to absorb, debate, question, and adapt this knowledge to present circumstances. This is a world of abstracts, sound bites, and great books that are, one is told, "skillfully condensed to heighten dramatic impact." It means little that the *purpose* held by the condensed author had little or nothing to do with dramatic impact. This high-speed environment demands a constant revelation of encapsulated truths and panaceas to add to the mounting megabytes of conventional wisdom. Our seats of learning have partly succumbed to the strident calls for change and in doing so have sacrificed the search for profound wisdom. Or perhaps they are no longer interested in producing graduates imbued with the desire to search for wisdom.

The quotation from Congreve at the head of the chapter would be politically unacceptable in today's society, but it does contain a germ of truth. It was also a harbinger of the direction that higher education was to take. Our schools, universities, and business colleges *do* exhibit a pedantic dedication to ensuring that students absorb a determined amount of facts and specific skills as the primary objective. This approach is designed to produce students who meet the prescribed requirements of the segmented and specialized outside world. This in itself is not wholly wrong, but it is more akin to training than to education. There is now no time for the "gentlemanly pursuit of knowledge," but in more prosaic terms "how to think" is being removed from the modern curriculum. It takes too long!

There is little evidence of *real* debate about the concepts behind the facts that are so diligently crammed. The traditional practice of debate and argument with each other and the tutor about what was being learned helped the student take ownership of concepts and establish his or her own set of values and principles. These values became the necessary horizons for subsequent thought and action. For example, increased emphasis on specialization has steadily eroded the concept of foundation subjects and the foundation year for professional degrees. Once upon a time, the student spent the last year at high school or the first year of college education devoted to such subjects as philosophy and logic. The aspiring architect spent a year studying general art and the nature of materials. The engineer and the surveyor spent their first year of higher education on a spread of twelve subjects that would include economics, common law, and other subjects not recognized as totally relevant to their specialization. There are many other examples of the foundation concept of higher education, or education to fit the participant to play a determinant part in society. These foundation subjects were once considered essential tools in learning to think to some purpose. They provided a perspective outside the specialization; more important, they instilled in the student the habit of asking questions. These questions were often answered by more questions, which in turn were answered by still other questions. To modern educators, much of this would seem a pointless exercise and a waste of the student's valuable time, which, they seem to believe, should be dedicated to the task of passing information-dominated exams. Yet arguably this approach was at the center of the Western world's most successful educational system. To those who experienced the process, it was a powerful route to greater understanding of the world we live in; though it has to be said that with its concomitant disciplines it was not always understood at the time. From the widest educational perspective, one can only lament, "Oh, my Jesuits of long ago."

Faculty and Students

All this mindless change in our educational systems has had its impact on the faculty and in turn on the students. From personal observation and anecdotal evidence, it would appear that much of the faculty (not unlike their brethren in the corporate chateaux) have become more introverted in their thinking and more selfish in their attitudes. Professors, teachers, and lecturers appear to be more conscious of the opportunities to exploit their position for personal gain or kudos than their responsibilities to their students. An increasing proportion of their time is dedicated to the publication of "prominent" papers or books, well-funded esoteric research, or lucrative TV spots or consulting. This is all to the detriment of their students to the extent that the lecture room is competing with the highly paid business seminar.

Looking back at personal experience, I feel that time spent with dedicated academics was always invigorating and rewarding. Despite all the excuses of busy schedules, it was time sought after. Today the experience remains interesting and can make for a lively lunch or dinner. However, something is missing, and in many cases it has been replaced by an unhealthy cynicism about the whole process. It seems that we are no longer celebrating the triumph of thought with some merry quip or amusing tales of the temerity of a student or another academic. A reflective port has been replaced with a sparkling champagne. Now we celebrate the latest "winning" of a research project involving travel to an exotic part of the globe or the latest royalty payment for a "*Business Week* best-seller." We used to respect them as the possessors of profound wisdom. Now they are just one of us.

The change in educational objectives and the attitude of tutors has had a profound effect on students. I was late into the field but have now had more than twenty years' experience educating and training business leaders, managers, and supervisors in a variety of business subjects. My judgments cannot be accepted as totally objective because they depend in part on my own effectiveness as a tutor. However, I have been shattered by what I perceive as the changes in the attitudes of students over the relatively short period of twenty years.

In the 1970s, all around the world, the lecture hall and the classroom were exciting amphitheaters of debate and sometimes conclusion. This was even true of Eastern Europe, most particularly Poland, which was all still under communist domination. Students were eager to be challenged and confident enough in their inherent ability to think and to answer back. The constant challenge was stimulating, and the tutor possibly learned as much from the exercise as did the student.

As a tutor, I first perceived a real difference in the early 1980s in Florida. Twenty-two students were sitting listening to an instructor as if he were proclaiming the latest pronouncements of an accepted god. They were not servile, but positively enthusiastic. They laughed in all the right places and at every break discussed the issues in terms of the power of the message. The instructor was good—but not that good. Nobody had the slightest inclination to argue the concepts. This evangelical course met some need for proclaimed truth or faith rather than the pursuit of knowledge. But hundreds of such courses were being held across the United States with similar results. The precommitted group had arrived. It wasn't that the concepts being taught were necessarily wrong but that the students were not questioning them; *this* was the issue. But here is the kicker: These students were all senior managers of leading U.S. corporations. Their earlier experience in college was now honed by their experience of corporate culture. They had learned that survival depended upon declaring enthusiasm for each corporate initiative. Questioning the concept came very close to treason. Students were conditioned, and few even recognized, let alone admitted, that they were prostituting their intellect. This attitude is probably a root cause for the high rate of failure in so many corporate initiatives.

In the middle 1980s, the same movement for change (its title was then Quality) reached Europe. Now instructors trained in the U.S. environment were facing European business students. These students hadn't been conditioned, so they argued, much to the amazement of their American tutors. Trying to explain to a U.S. lecturer that his most vociferous students would end up the most committed individuals at the end of the course was difficult. The concept that they were arguing because they were interested was almost impossible to get across. Even more difficult to grasp was the fact that every major European country argued from a different premise. The British were haughtily skeptical, the French used the power of logic to destroy argument, and the Germans wanted every detail of implementation explained. It is of interest these reactions were not automatically chauvinistic. The student reaction was a natural one to the teaching of new concepts and was similar whether the tutor was American or European.

By the late 1980s and into the 1990s, the atmosphere had changed. The pace of change in education and the growing globalization of business were standardizing student reaction around the world. There are both positive and negative aspects to this change. The business student in Calcutta, Harrisburg, London, Sydney, and Lagos approaches a business course or seminar with a similar attitude: "Yes, great concept—but let me have the workbook and the case histories." Universally, collection of facts has become more important than ideas. Around the world, managers and students have little time for what they call specious argument; they want action.

In this context, I reveal a secret ambition. As with everyone else, my values and opinions have evolved from my education, social connections, and the books I have read and the films I have watched. I have always found that the medium of film is a very powerful influence. My desire is to facilitate an executive workshop to evaluate the business lessons to be learned from the following films:

12 Angry Men
Paths of Glory
Judgment at Nuremberg
Inherit the Wind

In my opinion, most of the conceptual foundation for business values and principles is to be found in the arguments developed dramatically in those films. With some cynical amusement, I assert that a five-day workshop based on these films would provide a serious foundation course for modern managers.

Learning From History

It would be ludicrous to argue that our educational systems should return to those of the leisured period of Congreve. At that time, only a small proportion of the population received any education or training. But it would also be folly to ignore the educational lessons from the past. Today it is fashionable to say that there is little that we can learn from history because history never repeats itself exactly. The conclusion appears reasonable, but it is yet another illustration of the lazy thinking that permeates so much of modern education. It is highly unlikely that the *facts* of history or a particular situation repeat themselves. But it is almost certain that the *concepts* that caused the facts are repeated continuously. The student of history can well say, "Forget the facts; give me the truth." From the perspective of business education, the idea that we have little to learn from history is a dangerous fallacy.

This viewpoint can be demonstrated by examining two examples from military history. The American Civil War battle of Gettysburg and the naval battle of Jutland from World War I are both in the curricula of the military colleges of the United States and Europe. Both battles have been studied and written about in minute detail. There is probably little more to discover about the specific facts of the battles and the decisions made by all the competing commanders. All of these specific *facts* would be of little value *alone* as the basis for training future commanders. They are very unlikely to face the same juxtaposition of resources, technology, personalities, and terrain in their command situations. On the surface, there is no comparison in the context of today's battlefield. Yet both battles are still taught in the military schools of many countries. The reason for their educational importance is that both battles illustrate some essential *conceptual* lessons for the management of warfare. These concepts, learned from analysis of old-time battles, played a significant part in the education of recent successful commanders in the Falklands War and in Desert Storm in the Persian Gulf.

The military concepts involved are closely related to the management concepts employed by successful evolutionary companies. The misuse or ignorance of these concepts played a key part in the defeat of Gen. Robert E. Lee at Gettysburg and the opportunities for victory lost by Adm. John Rushworth Jellico at Jutland. These concepts that override mere facts can be summarized in the following discussions.

A Clear Purpose

This is the essential element to both military and business success. At Gettysburg, the Southern armies had divided objectives (unlike their previous forays into the North) and their commander was ill and communicated with little clarity. At Jutland, the British admiral had little sense of purpose and in reality was merely parading great battleships in line and expecting the enemy to run away.

Prime Minister Thatcher portrayed a very clear sense of purpose in the Falklands conflict. Her strength of purpose overrode all the doubts of the British military, the U.S. State Department, and the United Nations.

Thatcher was again involved with President George Bush in establishing clarity of purpose in the Gulf conflict, in bringing diverse nations to share the purpose of the Gulf War.

Understanding the Other Side of the Hill

This military concept has always permeated the great military commanders and the leaders of industry. It goes beyond mere military intelligence.

Many of Lee's victories were based on an intuitive feeling for this concept. At Gettysburg this was all lost. His own illness slowed his reactions to what was happening and the total irresponsibility of his subordinate Gen. Jeb Stuart deprived Lee of the information that he had expected.

At Jutland, Admiral Jellico, and to some extent Admiral David Beatty, his second in command, had little or no interest in the capability or tactics of the German High Seas Fleet.

In the Falklands and the Gulf War, new developments such as the Exocet and Iraqi missiles caused some unforeseen dilemmas. But in essence, the superior intelligence gathering of the Western commanders and their conceptual use of that intelligence allowed them to maximize their military potential.

Concentration of Force

Concentration of force or firepower to maximum advantage is one of the most essential elements in the training of military personnel. Concentration of key competencies on market targets is a similar business concept.

The study of the battle of Gettysburg illustrates to modern students how General Lee missed two, and possibly three, opportunities to concentrate his forces in time and disposition to win the battle.

At Jutland, Admiral Jellico missed three opportunities to "cross the T" (the naval version of concentration of force) or concentrate his battleship firepower on the advancing line of German ships. In the simple but powerful words of Winston Churchill, "When all is said and done, three times is a lot."

With totally different circumstances and technologies, the British in the Falklands (and to more effect the Allies in the Gulf) showed a complete mastery of this concept in the air, on land, and at sea.

Outflanking the Enemy's Concentration

This classic principle of war is known to every commander. To bring one's power to bear where it is least expected and thus destroy your enemy from the side or from behind is an obvious objective in warfare. So too in business, this is not easy to achieve if only for the reason that every enemy expects you to try. The constraints to achieving success may be enemy dispositions, terrain, time, and weather.

Lee, until then the master of the battlefield, failed to apply all the key concepts to the extent that he probably didn't even realize the opportunities for total victory available to him through outflanking his enemy. One of his commanders, Gen. James Longstreet, did realize it, but out of loyalty to Lee he did not press his views to the point of no return. First General John Buford, and then Lieutenant Colonel Joshua L. Chamberlain (the real victors of Gettysburg) with their speed of reaction and incredible bravery obscured the possibilities for Lee.

Jellico didn't even understand the concept. His handling of the battle cruisers (and his difficult subordinate Beatty) totally ignored the real possibility of denying the German fleet a way home.

An outflanking movement was achieved in the Falklands, but its determination owed more to other decision criteria than as the prime objective.

Gen. Norman Schwartzkopf's land and air strategies were exemplary and produced a classic exposition of this concept. Desert Storm will play a major part in the military schools of the

future. One short war is probably not enough to place Schwartzkopf's handling of the battlefield on a par with the brilliance
of Patton and Rommel, but for a few days in the Gulf he was
undoubtedly in their company.

Back to Business

These concepts (together with some others) are vital to success
in warfare. But military schools, like business schools, are dominated by the current conventional wisdom. As in business, this
wisdom is based on views of, say, the dominant role of cavalry or
of quality being an expensive option rather than the core of the
concept. Business schools are also more likely to teach the concept or the lessons of history through *educational* conventional
wisdom: the case-history method.

The case-history method of education certainly helps the
student understand the concepts involved, but usually within the
tight constraints of the problems posed. For example, in the military context we have been discussing, the military students re-
fight the battles of Gettysburg and Jutland from the perspective
of the original battlefields. The best teams of students demonstrate a high degree of perception and understanding of the concepts taught. They produce plans that appear far more credible
and would have been more successful than the actual decisions
of Lee and Jellico. They have understood the concept but have
only applied it with the hindsight of history and in the defined
environment. They have solved an ancient problem but are not
necessarily equipped to handle a new one.

Next time, Buford will be hesitant, Chamberlain will with-
draw, and there will also not be a Cemetery Ridge! How then do
we act?

Using the lessons of history merely to replay history and
solve the initial problems is a pointless exercise. To use these
lessons to understand these concepts as the basis for outside-
the-box scenarios is a very powerful educational tool. In the military analogy, the student could visualize the airplane as an element of outflanking, or modern communications capability as an
element of the concept of concentration of force. In other words,
the educational issue is to encourage debate, questioning, and

thinking centered on the *concepts* rather than the details of implementation. Those with the ability to perceive the unthinkable drive the future.

These military analogies may seem to be outside the subject, but there are aspects of current military training that do provide lessons for the business community. Many leaders of industry who experienced the training and management methods of the military of earlier decades are likely to consider the words *military intelligence* as a perfect oxymoron. To that generation, military culture could be summed up by "if it moves, salute it; if it stands still, paint it." But there has been an evolutionary change in the development of military leaders. Led by the Israeli Army and the SAS (Strategic Air Services) elements of the British Army, militaries worldwide have been applying conceptual intelligence and awareness to training their soldiers. Anyone involved in selling to the military in the middle 1970s recognized the development of a very different kind of colonel or brigadier. Those young commanders discussed their management issues in terms of advanced business principles. They recognized (ahead of their business contemporaries) that modern technology outdated the conventional wisdom of maintaining the unthinking military discipline of the guards or marines regiments would no longer work. A commodore in the Indian Air Force put it to me succinctly. "John, we have just paid $23 million for this airplane; it flies at 2,300 kph, and the airman flying it is only twenty-three years old. Suddenly, we realized that we couldn't order him to send us a memo before he made a decision. We had discovered empowerment." We return to these issues in Chapter 12.

Business Schools

Business schools and university schools of management have a lot to answer for in the context of current management practice. As one might expect, there are both positive and negative elements in their relationship with business and public-sector organizations.

On the positive side, they provide centers of learning in the sense that they support some substantial leaders of thought in the management field. They are also the source for disciplined research into many aspects of knowledge. They have sought and received sponsorship from the world of business. There are numerous examples from around the world of close-working and successful partnerships between business and academia that have been to the advantage of both, and indeed to the community at large.

Collaborating with partners outside the campus may appear to be a healthy, positive, extroverted involvement designed to broaden perspective. In actuality, much of this activity has become an introverted activity to the detriment of the primary purpose. Some of this external work does involve students, particularly postgraduate students. However, the majority of this work is for the benefit of the individual members of the faculty. But the primary purpose of universities and business colleges is to educate students to play a constructive role in enhancing our society—more specifically herein, in managing future organizations. There are substantial questions to be answered in how effectively our centers of learning carry out their primary role.

Over recent years, mass production of M.B.A.s of dubious distinction has been the subject of criticism in both the United States and Europe. This rote-based approach to producing business managers exhibits some of the worst elements in Japanese business education. In chasing a Western repetition of Japanese success, we are too prone to adopting some Eastern practices without adaptive thought. We also fail to notice that Japanese business leaders are themselves expressing considerable concern about the products of their own educational systems. This approach to business education was one of the reasons for the relative failure of the TQM movement in the eighties. Disciplined prescriptive answers to the problems of business and management are no substitute for thinking managers empowered to think the unthinkable.

Perhaps the most pernicious element in the development of business school methodology has been the Harvard Business School case history. A constant stream of these case histories and their like have dominated business schools and external seminars for decades. They have engendered the belief that there is always a ready-made solution for every business issue. All we need to do is find the relevant case history. For years, the conventional wisdom of Harvard has been successfully promoted as though it had the authority of God. This has not been a problem for the business environment because it has got into the habit of accepting false gods.

Western business is now questioning this approach to the higher education of business entrants. In fairness to Harvard University, it should also be noted that leading members of their faculty have expressed their own concern with the case-history approach. Unfortunately, the perceived authority of Harvard has permeated business education across the globe. In recent years, I have conducted tutorials or seminars in eastern Europe, India, Africa, and the Middle East. The business students from these recent entrant nations to capitalism are avid seekers of knowledge from the market economies. Without fail, they all ask for masses of documentation and case histories. As a matter of educational principle, I refuse to provide case histories and explain why. The aim of business education is to introduce the students to concepts and then to provide them with the opportunity for argument and rigorous thought about the *concept*, not its application. The participants should be led to take personal ownership of the ideas so that they can more readily *adapt* them to their own culture and business situation. Most of them are emerging from perhaps fifty years of a totalitarian culture. The last thing that will help them on their journey is another prescriptive solution from a substitute guru.

The challenge for our educational system is most certainly to raise standards of both teaching and results in terms of student exam performance. But if all of this were achieved, it would all be of little significance for the long-term benefit of society if there is no provision—or *permission*—for argument and thought. Perhaps a practical route would be through the curricula, in attempt to ensure that there is greater inclusion of *foundation* elements.

Corporate Education and Training

There is a significant differential in the approach of evolutionary companies and others to developing their people. All the successful companies noted in this book place high priority on this aspect of their cultural strategies and operational tactics. It is also important to realize that in this context *development* encompasses more than provision of education and training. Recruitment policies, induction programs, foundation programs, opportunities to practice theory, and the important "permissions" to take risks in action are all part of this wider management development process. Perhaps the strongest evidence of the impact of their holistic approach is the *fact* that evolutionary companies rarely look outside the corporation for a new chief executive officer. The career path of Jack Welch, one of the most internationally renowned of CEOs, is a case in point.

In contrast, the majority of organizations foster very different attitudes amongst their people. Corporate leaders loudly lament the falling standards they perceive in the management school entrants from higher education. In the same breath, they pride themselves on increasing their investment in a new training program to redress the situation. But in reality they are once again wallowing in quick-fix moonshine. They portray little evidence of applied thought in trying to analyze the root causes of the "gimme" attitudes of their potential leaders, which, if uncorrected, can perpetrate great damage to the corporation.

Despite current employment insecurity, the well-*qualified* graduate arrives in the selected corporation with an attitude that he or she knows everything (just look at my grades) and expect immediate entry to the fast track. These graduates have little patience with corporate procedures and want early involvement in high salaries, fast promotion, and all the perks of corporate officers. They have arrived with a corporate chateau mentality inculcated at business school. There are positive aspects to this attitude, which, if channeled or disciplined, could be powerful drivers in developing innovation and initiative. In too many companies, the entry attitude is meekly accepted if not actively encouraged. As a result, hundreds of other hard-working employees are left to shrug their shoulders and wonder if all their dedicated application over the years was worth the effort. Any new employee who persists with such an entry attitude at Procter and Gamble, Arthur Andersen, 3M, or Marks and Spencer receives very short shrift. Perhaps more to the point, they probably wouldn't be recruited in the first place.

There is another example of mindless change in the development of future managers. The rapid demise of the concept of "articled pupil" in professional areas (as it is known in the UK) and of apprenticeship in manufacturing has happened without much thought to its replacement. It is true that both practices have deteriorated into varying forms of cheap labor without offering enough compensatory advantages to the recipient. Yet these approaches to induction provide a thorough grounding in the corporate culture and the marriage between theory and experience. In combination with the steady erosion of the foundation year or broader school curriculum, these changes have removed an essential steadying influence on the development of young managers. Interestingly, evolutionary companies have given thought to this area, and we examine their answers to the dilemma in later chapters.

In essence, the argument in this chapter probably depends on the reader's selection of either dictionary definition of the word *conservative*, namely, (1) opposition to change and innovation or (2) a philosophy advocating the preservation of the *best* of the established order in society.

Those who see *conservative* in the first definition have little truck with those who caution more thought and thus drive forward change and innovation for the sake of change alone. In so doing, this conservative believes that much is sacrificed. Modern business education and the development of managers exhibit those tendencies. We need a new commitment to lifelong learning at the workplace.

Consultants and Gurus

The knowledgeable outsider *does* have a positive role to play in helping any organization achieve success. The highly specialized consultant provides in-depth knowledge not available inside the company. The consultant's role is likely to expand as companies reengineer their processes and make the strategic decision not to be the masters of everything. There is some justice in that many of these consultants were earlier victims of downsizing in the very same corporations. The effectiveness of the more generalist consultant depends on the core mission or attitude of each side of the partnership in considering any specific project.

The client who reacts in desperation to a perceived crisis

and calls for help from a consultant, or who has reacted to the clarion call of the latest management guru, is in trouble. The crisis has obscured judgment and the consultant tends to be viewed as some kind of savior. In business, it is an axiom that instant conversion to a new faith has a pernicious effect on executive decisions. Vast sums are spent with consultants and gurus used as *substitute decision makers*. Swarms of lesser consultants soon suck the pollen from the organization and play havoc with the company's culture and its people.

On the other hand, the consultant who views his or her role as giving the client *ownership* of their knowledge so that they are enabled to create their own success can be a powerful asset. These consultants help the client adapt outside perspectives to improve their own practices and processes. There are more consultants of such responsibility around than is generally recognized.

It is interesting to compare the impact of success on the business guru and the political leader. Both are susceptible to the corruption of power and in both cases often succumb. But there does seem to be a distinct difference between the business guru and the political leader in the manner in which they use and exploit their success. To some extent, both are children of the media. The political achiever usually *intends* to be a leader from the outset and so has a tendency to mature into the role. The guru has usually stumbled into the limelight by the accident of a timely book or TV interview. Gurus tend to be less well prepared for the fame and attention. Soon they begin to believe all the hype and see themselves as the carrier of a great message for the benefit of their fellows. But under pressure they are likely to exhibit an underlying lack of confidence and maturity, with displays of arrogance or petulance. Examples from each arena illustrate the difference.

Margaret Thatcher was a conviction politician with a very strong belief in herself and her opinions. Contrary to many published comments, she was interested in other *informed* opinion whether or not it was in total agreement with her own. She was intolerant of uninformed opinion or indecisive delays designed to thwart her direction. I have a letter from Lady Thatcher that contains the sentence, "I think it was fortunate for history that Ronald Reagan, Mr. Gorbachev, and I were in power at the same time." From anyone else, this statement would be deemed the height of arrogance. From Margaret Thatcher, it is a statement of fact; her letter goes on to say "It is a pity that the electoral cycle was such that we could not finish the task to which we had set our hands." There is a sense of belief and character in these sentences that mark a leader.

By the nature of my work, I have had contact with a number of business gurus; I worked for one, Philip Crosby. With the possible exception of Joseph Juran (he remains a charming gentleman who always appears to have time for other opinions), all were egocentrics. Crosby certainly could be a charming and humorous host if the mood took him, but he did not like argument. One incident sticks in my mind. We were attending a management meeting of his company, PCA, at which there was some debate about a new video product. As usual, the video was dominated by Philip Crosby, but that attracted no argument. None of those present would have dared. To my mind, the video contained too many examples drawn from U.S. sports such as baseball and American football. The fact that the rest of the world did not play and knew little about these sports was detrimental to their intended message in the international market. No doubt my argument was pressed to the extreme, but it was ended by a typical Philip Crosby interjection: "The elephant sits where it wants to sit." My attempt at having the last word, "It is difficult to be creative when dodging elephants from chair to chair," received the definitive Crosby riposte: "John, yours is not the creative role." In view of what Crosby taught, and accepting all my own catalogue of faults, that seemed intellectual arrogance in the extreme. I owe Philip Crosby a lot in opening my mind to other ideas, and he was in most ways a considerate and caring employer, but that was enough; it was the moment I decided to resign from PCA.

Most business soothsayers see their own little vision as the complete answer to the problems of business. In most cases, there is a nucleus of profound wisdom or enlightening common sense in their proclamations. Actually, the idea probably started that way with them, but the ego and adulation expand the idea into a new faith. One crucial mistake that business gurus tend to make is to underestimate the power of the existing culture in every organization. Cultures or value systems (good or bad) are deeply involved in the perceptions of employees, customers, and suppliers in every decision. For example, in retrospect we can see that Philip Crosby's greatest mistake was in misunderstanding the power of this culture. This in part accounts for the relative failure of TQM in the eighties. He argued, effectively, that the success of Japan (then the current major competitor) had little or nothing to do with culture. His point was that Japan's five-thousand-year-old culture had produced rubbish until only a few years ago, so culture was not an element in their success.

Crosby's own distillation of their success was based on four absolutes of quality and fourteen steps for implementation. Thousands of companies around the world followed his powerful lead word for word and tried to implement his absolutes and steps. The concepts had validity, and many companies improved. But only those who understood their own culture and *adapted* the concepts to their own culture were really successful. Crosby's solutions for the competitive issues facing Western business were partly right, but only if implemented in the evolutionary pattern determined by individual company cultures.

Questions for the Reader

1. Did your schooling start the process of thinking for you?
2. Did school and college equip you for the workplace?
3. Can you remember specific tutors who seemed to make learning come alive and be a joy?
4. Which philosophy or special sensual delight has permeated your whole life? Did it originate in school, in college, or from a friend?
5. How exciting were your early days at work?
6. Have you experienced the help of a mentor at college or in business ? Did it make a difference?
7. Try to list for yourself from your own experience the positive and negative elements in your education and training at school, college, and work.
8. Do you have a personal development plan? If so, was it prepared of your own volition or in collaboration with your employers?
9. Note your own reactions to consultants and gurus. How do they compare with those expressed in this book?
10. Do you enjoy your work?

Part Two

Pause for Thought

These middle chapters examine the real nature of change. They indicate that change is not as dramatic as proclaimed and that it certainly does not move at the pace that it is currently fashionable to believe.

This century has witnessed momentous change, but it could be argued that we are now in and can anticipate a reasonably long period of stability. In the perspective of history, these are not tumultuous years.

Chapter 6

Anticipating Change

I hesitate to say what the functions of the modern journalist may be; but I imagine that they do not exclude the intelligent anticipation of facts even before they do occur.

Lord Curzon (1859–1925)

The most reliable way to anticipate the future is by understanding the present.

John Naisbitt

My interest is in the future; I am going to spend the rest of my life there.

Charles Kettering

Curiosity killed the cat, but lack of curiosity may have killed the dinosaur.

John Macdonald

Time present and time past
Are both perhaps present in time future
And time future contained in time past.

T. S. Eliot (1888–1965)

To be able to anticipate change and to manage the future, we must first be able to understand the present. Yet most of the time we are so caught up in the activities of the present that we do not observe the reality of what is going on around us. In general, we absorb what we want to see; we are programmed to see or have the training or ability to see. As a result, we do not understand what is happening now. With this limited focus, we have no foundation for recognizing changes or trends and their possible interrelationships at the time that they are happening. But the congruence of these evolutionary changes determines our future and the perpetuity of our corporations.

It is time to count the greens. Art students are taught an exercise to help develop their powers of observation. They are asked to look at a landscape or garden and then count the number of different shades of green that they can see. Color, to the eye, is only the reflection of light from different surfaces; therefore the variety of color to be seen depends upon the time of day, the season, and the level of light and shade. However, the focused mind should be able to use its eyes to see about seventeen shades of green in normal circumstances. This *focused* approach to looking helps the art student (or anyone else for that matter) understand that there is more to see than is at first envisaged. In this chapter, we examine aspects of developing focus and perspective to understand what is happening around us that will help grow our businesses for the future.

Perspective

Perspective and focus are two factors in developing understanding of what is happening. To a large extent, what we see and understand is determined by our own perspective. Many of the failures of corporate management to perceive the change around it is the result of limitations on its perspective. Focus is essentially an act of the intellect and can be used to widen perspective, as in our example of counting the greens. Managed focus is a characteristic of evolutionary companies (so we return to this factor later). Perspective is more subject to the emotional side of our thinking processes. Each individual's *natural* perspective (as distinct from a taught and developed perspective) is the result of influences from a number of sources.

Consideration of these influences and sources is an important element in comprehending why generally held opinions on the degree and pace of change are wrong. These influences on an overall perspective could be defined in a number of ways, but three areas suffice to develop the key points: (1) time and place, (2) power and position, and (3) experience and knowledge.

Time and Place

Gurus and consultants promoting their latest book, product, or seminar are prone to use such phrases as "these tumultuous years" and "a radically changing world." Dire consequences are forecast for those companies that do not react to the "ever growing pace of change." These pronouncements influence the perspective of many individuals, but they would be wiser to first widen their own perspective of their own time and place.

Are these really tumultuous years? If you currently live and work in Bosnia, Afghanistan, Iraq, and several African states, you might well describe these as tumultuous years. But is the statement really true of the United States and most of Europe? In fact, the evidence is that rather than this being an "age of instability," to quote Price Pritchett, we may well be entering a long period of relative stability not unlike that experienced in Europe following the defeat of Napoleon.

All these terms are comparative and are again related to time and place. Most Europeans would recognize certain periods in recent centuries as being tumultuous: the age of revolutions from 1776 to 1805; the First World War and its immediate aftermath (1914–1920); followed by its later result, the rise of Fascism; and the broad Second World War period (1933–1948). For people living then in the United States, some of those periods (though of much shorter duration) were seen in a similar light but they might have added the 1860s, the time of the Civil War, as very tumultuous. The latter event was hardly noticed by the Europeans of the period.

The *pace* of change is also relative to the perspective of time and place. The current use of the phrase "accelerating pace of change" generally relates to technological change and its impact on the way we live and work. But it is arguable that the impact on the way of life brought about by successive inventions of the railroad, the automobile, and the airplane was, at certain stages in the development of each, much greater and happened at a faster pace. In the context of place, a perspective on all these changes would be relatively similar in Europe, Japan, and the United States. It would be seen very differently from the perspective of Russians, Chinese, Africans, and many South Americans.

Power and Position

An individual's perspective of the world of change has always been affected by position on the ladder of power. Power may be derived from hierarchical position in the organization, social position, or some form of political or financial influence. For example, the Depression in the early 1930s in the United States influenced the perspective of every American. But the perspective of this event for the Oklahoma farmer is likely to be radically different to that of the Boston Brahmin. In a similar manner, a communist has a radically different perspective from that of a capitalist on almost every issue.

To an extent, these examples point out the obvious because they illustrate extremes. But there are countless graduations of these perspectives that lead to differing views of how to manage change. At the extreme, the world has been bedeviled by these conflicts. In the world of business, the conflicts between the perspectives of "them and us" is still a formidable barrier to overall "win-win" evolutionary change.

Experience and Knowledge

Our experience and knowledge have a major influence on our perspective. Interestingly, each can lead to a closed or an open perspective. For example, twenty years' experience can sometimes truthfully be described as one year's experience of doing the same thing twenty times. That could lead to an ever-narrowing perspective. Alternatively, it could represent twenty years of an ever-broadening experiencing of the world and thus to a much more open perspective.

Knowledge is affected similarly. Lack of knowledge, if it is accidental to the issue, can lead to curiosity and questioning. In that case, it is a positive contribution to perspective. More usually, lack of knowledge provides limitations and inhibitions that tend to close perspective. Conversely, detailed knowledge can lead to specialization and closing of perspectives. But it is more usual for knowledge to be a key to greater understanding.

From the standpoint of this book, experience and knowledge can be managed and focused to contribute to the success of organizations. We return to this facet in the last section of this chapter, where we develop the ability to focus.

Revolution or Evolution

The fashionable "revolutionary changes" in business are nothing of the sort. They are but distinct phases in clearly recognizable evolutions. All were identified, anticipated, and acted upon by evolutionary companies. However, it is true that these evolutions have had revolutionary impact on particular corporations and public organizations. Almost without exception, these were groups that had failed to understand the present and so were unable to anticipate change. In a few cases, individual leaders wilfully ignored the evidence of change to suit their own selfish short-term aims. In both the business and the political arena, events caught up with the managers and brought forth an intense period of mindless change.

To help understand the nature and pace of change, let us briefly consider two evolutionary changes which were pretty well completed before most people had noticed. Both are technology developments that have had a profound impact on the way in which we live and work. If they were "new" today, our relish of the buzzword would probably make them part of the "internal climate revolution." Let us identify them more prosaically: central heating and air conditioning. Both of these applied evolutions also illustrate the influence of time and place on our perspective of change.

The Romans mastered the concept of central heating for their major public buildings; today central heating is common in public buildings throughout the world. Apart from attracting itinerants to public libraries during cold spells and making work or public events tolerable, it has had little impact on our social life. But its relatively recent introduction to the home has had a profound impact.

Central heating was rare in British homes before the 1960s. It was introduced much earlier into the harsher and richer climes of the United States and Canada. Outside Europe and North America, central heating is still relatively rare in the private home. Central heating has destroyed the family unit as we once understood it, and as some still nostalgically visualize it. In the days of radiated heat from a coal, gas, or electric fire, the family gathered around the one central source of comfort. Only the rich could afford to have a fire lit in every room. (Incidentally, central heating should be more accurately described as distributed heating.) This close-knit communal living for one-half the year determined the hierarchical choice of activity within the heated living room. Generally, dad decided what board game would be played or what radio program would be selected. A dutiful mother and children were environmentally programmed to accept and indeed delight in this command-and-control culture. These ingrained habits naturally extended far beyond the living room. Dads were obeyed.

Central heating changed all that. Individual members of the family could disappear to the far corners of the house and make independent decisions as to how to spend their time. For a period, the lure of television held the pass for dad, but now computers and CD-ROMs are in all the "kids" rooms. Of course, there were other influences at work, not least the increased buying power of the young, but central heating broke the ingrained family habits of generations.

For the majority, air conditioning in the home is still confined to North America. More temperate climates or economic wealth have placed air conditioning fairly low in the priorities for the family budget. However, like central heating, air conditioning is common in public buildings across the world (though often of dubious efficiency). But the economic availability of air conditioning for most homes has transformed many areas of the United States. Apart from the accident of birth, relatively few would *choose* to live in some of the southern states of the United States without air conditioning. The advent of air conditioning (in congruence with some other changes affecting mobility) has played a major part in the rapid expansion of many areas in Florida and in Atlanta, Phoenix, and other cities. Air conditioning has created a mass migration from the North to the South comparable to the earlier drive West.

Evolving Markets

Many companies follow the evolutionary growth of specialized markets. They do not feel the need for explosive growth and depend less on boom cycles. They compete in stable markets but grow across international boundaries as their chosen market migrates. They play the long-term plan with small markets that they know will grow. They are managed by practical, down-to-earth managers who exhibit close attention to detail and the realities of change.

Some of these companies are substantial by any measurement, but in general they measure their progress in market share. Many are medium-sized companies, often family owned, and like their larger brethren in the world-class evolutionary companies they almost all have strong value systems. In the main, these companies do not seek publicity and so are little known to the general public even though they dominate their own markets. A few selected from an article in *UK Director* magazine by Hermann Simon in October 1996 are good examples:

- Hauni: the world market leader in cigarette manufacturing machines. Hauni has a world market share of nearly 90 percent in high-speed cigarette machines
- Baader: owns 90 percent of the world market for fish processing machines
- Webasto: the world leader in both sunroofs and auxiliary heating systems for cars
- Stihl: a highly innovative company in the chainsaw market that claims a global share close to 30 percent, double that of its closest competitor in a major consumer market
- Wurth: by far the largest supplier of assembly products in the world, with its strongest competitor about one fifth the size; operates in forty-four countries and continues to grow and strengthen its lead

All of these companies take great pains to understand exactly what is happening today in their markets so as to better anticipate the future. None of them have needed reengineering or internal revolutions. They have highly committed and trained managers with the ability to act on a sure footing in the global marketplace.

Six Evolutions to Watch

One facet of mindless change that was noted earlier is the tendency for executives to leap upon a single issue or concept as the total answer to their problems. There may well be a substantial element of common sense in the concept, but it cannot provide a whole solution. Success, failure, and change are holistic results of several converging movements, be they evolutionary or revolutionary.

There are six distinct but linked evolutions that influence the nature of business, the structure of organizations, and the behavior and attitude of managers and workers alike. Figure 6-1 represents these six evolutions as linked circles, highlighting the interaction between each and all, centered around the future, which they help shape. Understanding the nature and effects of these evolutions helps companies anticipate and make decisions for a holistic future.

The Demographic Evolution

Substantial changes are taking place in the composition of populations across the world. These changes are bound to affect both the nature of work and the migration of some industries across or among continents. Though the movement differs from nation to nation, it can be broadly summarized as a major reduction in birth rates in the advanced or wealthier nations, falling infant mortality rates in the poorer nations, and rapidly improving longevity in the wealthy nations, all of which are changing population numbers and the balance between young and old.

Economic pressure at home in the poorer countries and the advent of relatively cheap or easy travel have created new migratory patterns. Recent political changes in Eastern Europe are pro-

Figure 6-1. The six evolutions.

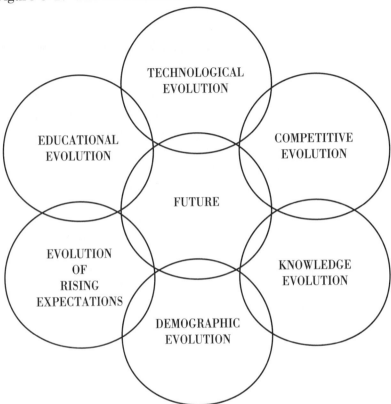

moting more major population migrations. Increasingly, the richer nations are resorting to tougher immigration controls. However, if people do not migrate, then industry, particularly but not exclusively manufacturing industry, will migrate in pursuit of the people and cheaper labor rates. All these movements are well advanced and are already changing the service-versus-manufacturing mix in richer nations.

The Competitive Evolution

The evolution of the global economy could be said to have begun with the Japanese invasion of Western markets. Once labeled as the quality revolution, it is now clear that a much broader evolution was at hand. This evolution is inextricably intertwined with the collapse of collectivism and intellectual acceptance of the "market-led economy or society." These combined evolutions clearly influence the thinking of managers in both the commercial and the public sectors. It has a steady and massive influence on society as a whole. Already, whole nations are under the influence of the competitive evolution, and it clearly embraces service sectors such as health care and government agencies. The worldwide competitive evolution is the stimulant for much of the change that indubitably abounds and for the evolution of rising expectations. We look more closely at the competitive evolution in Chapter 8.

The Evolution of Rising Expectations

Rising expectations are not confined to the Third World or to straitened economic circumstances. This evolution takes many forms, but it is present in almost all societies. With some people, it may be confined to lifting their heads above mere survival; with others it is expressed in terms of quality of life or perhaps a more focused desire to determine their individual destinies. This may prove to be the most powerful of all the evolutions in modifying the structure and managerial principles of future organizations in sophisticated economies.

I well remember my first experience and understanding of this evolution in practice back in the middle seventies. I was then employed by one of the world's leading corporations. Employees who were motivated to advance and who were recognized by the company as having potential were required to expand their experience and prove their worth in the far-flung outposts of the corporate empire. In American terms, this might involve running the UK operation. In British terms, it would involve managing Scotland, Ireland, or the Northern Region of England. The potential leaders would disappear to their respective colonial outposts of the corporate empire; the best quickly proved themselves and were invited back to substantial promotions on the corporate ladder. But in the interim, something had changed. They and their families had discovered the quality of life. Land, stables, countryside, and minimal commuting had established a new set of personal values. One might ask, "Why on earth do I need to go through all the stresses of central corporate or big city life when I have everything here I need for the good life?" The corporation may bewail those persons' lack of ambition or their loss of the "killer instinct." But the corporation was wrong; they had just replaced one ambition with another ambition.

Increasingly, intelligent and ambitious workers and managers are demanding a greater say in their business destinies and their quality of life. In Britain, there have been cynical comments about not being able to stand the heat in the kitchen directed at politicians who resigned for the express reason of spending more time with their families. High-pressure working may have been a contributory factor in their decision, but it could be wiser for the future of our organizational practices to take their explanations at face value. Obvious technical talent and leadership potential cannot be squandered on the altar of corporate procedures rooted in tradition. Successful organizations will be those who master all the implications of the evolution of rising expectations. Link this train of thinking with the individual mobility provided by the technological evolution, and a new free-form organizational structure evolves and finally replaces the typical authoritarian pyramid.

The Technology Evolution

The pace of technological change this century has been breathtaking, everyone agrees, and it is still accelerating. On the surface, that statement appears to run counter to a key theme of this book. But there is an interesting paradox at the heart of change. As we absorb each change, we ourselves are changed and it becomes difficult to visualize our lives before the change came about. Try explaining to grandchildren what the world was like before cars, planes, telephones, television, computers, and ATMs. Yet none of these existed at the start of the Industrial Revolution, and even within the lifetime of some of us now. Equally, consider the effect on our grandchildren. Do they appear to be fazed by these incredible changes and totally lost in this new technological world? No; they take to it like a duck to water. The evident truth is that we adapt to change, and the changes themselves provide the ability to handle its pace and enormity.

It is not the purpose of this book to sit like King Canute and command the tide of change to reverse or even slow down. Rather, it is to argue that there is no need to panic and resort to mindless change. In Chapter 7, we examine this paradox further and hopefully demonstrate that we are capable of anticipating change and adapting to it with relative ease.

The Educational Evolution

At the turn of this century, the needs of industry (as discerned by Henry Ford and the control ethic) were actually based on a reduction of individual skills and thinking in the workforce. The corporate chateau was born with the organized division of employees into thinkers and doers. The evolution of technology and the increasing complexity of work processes have now put that trend into reverse. More and more, the robotic tasks of early industrialized workers have been taken over by technology. But control of these processes and technology has required an increasingly skilled and thinking workforce of collaborating management and workers.

Quite apart from the needs of industry, social changes have provided ever-widening educational opportunities for all levels of society. At its best, education stimulates thought and provokes a challenging attitude to many political and management practices. Educated workers are less likely to remain compliant to the same extent. It is interesting to conjecture whether the rise of dissidents that in part led to the collapse of Communism was the result of the general rise in education in the USSR or of the very high levels of education and training required of scientists and technologists in furtherance of technology. Education and training of all the population is becoming a priority of survival. But in anticipating and planning for this evolution, it would be dangerous to sacrifice quality for quantity. Developing and improving educational standards should be a major priority. A familiar axiom is worth repeating: It is more profitable to evaluate the cost of ignorance rather than the price of education.

Another aspect of the educational evolution relates to the changing position of women noted in the evolution of rising expectations. In Britain, more than 50 percent of university graduates are women. It is also true that some 40 percent of them, as desperately needed educated resources, leave industry and commerce within seven years. These evolutions require substantial changes in management thinking and practice. Provision of day care and flexible working hours are a very minor application of the new attitudes demanded to manage this aspect of tomorrow's business. Throughout the world, however sophisticated the economy, command and control is still dominated by male chauvinism, albeit often unconsciously. The whole attitude of senior male management can be summed up in an apocryphal quote: "It is very unfair to treat women as equals; it only confuses them."

The Knowledge Evolution

The rise in influence of the knowledge worker is already one of the most significant evolutions that are changing the nature of work and the way it is organized. The knowledge evolution is enabled by the technology evolution, is closely linked to the educational evolution, and acts as a driver in the evolution of rising expectations. Again, as one might expect, evolutionary companies are in the lead in experimenting in this aspect of business. Procter and Gamble is a recognized leader in the field.

Little more than a decade ago, knowledge workers were unique groups that didn't fit in with the culture of the majority. They were not interested in management issues or teamwork and often dressed differently to demonstrate their uniqueness. Now in some corporations they are in the majority, highly empowered and self-managed but learning to work in teams. They are reshaping the organization.

The initial self-directed teams were groups of knowledgeable generalists reskilled to work together, in many cases with the objective of reducing dependence on the individualistic, highly paid specialist. But the growing importance of technology reverses that trend. Increasingly, work is organized into knowledge work teams. These are groups of highly skilled specialists who operate in both the office and the factory. This method of working is steadily becoming distributed, even working together in locations across the globe. This evolution requires fundamental changes in personnel policies and the previous pattern of developing people through education and training. The evolution of the knowledge work team profoundly affects the way we work.

The impact of this evolution is well described in an intriguing and thought-provoking book, *The Distributed Mind*, by Kimball Fisher and Mareen Duncan Fisher. The Fishers describe their widespread research into the growth of knowledge work teams and identify six key trends in the workplace as the evolution continues, namely:

1. *Automation of physical work*: In the future, physical work on the shop floor and elsewhere will be done by machines, not people. Everyone has to learn how to be effective knowledge workers.

2. *Elimination of traditional jobs and work structures*: Many jobs, hierarchies, and bureaucracies will just disappear. Work and jobs will increasingly become project based, changing continuously.

3. *Empowered knowledge workers*: These workers will change relations at work. Managers of the future must coach, inform, and coordinate rather than direct.

4. *Domination of knowledge work teams*: This will be the dominating organizing unit because the technical sophistication of projects is so great that effective supervision by an individual is unlikely.

5. *Workplace flexibility*: Technology allows work to be done almost anywhere and doesn't require that it be done in an office or at a fixed location. Contrary to fashionable opinion, the Fishers do not believe that in the future the majority of work will be done at home. Their research into the attitudes of those involved in knowledge teams identifies other motivations that make this unlikely.

6. *Virtual knowledge teams*: This trend is related to the last one. Work won't be done in a single office with the same team of people anymore. Fewer and fewer workers work for one company full-time. A lifetime career inside one company will be extremely rare in the future.

Convergence

These parallel evolutions do not exist as distinct patterns of change that stand alone. Additionally, within each noted evolution there are distinct streams. For example, there are many aspects to technological change. As we have noted earlier, they are all interacting with and to some extent stimulating each other. They are easier to understand through observation and research when defined as distinct elements. However, the most fruitful area for consideration when anticipating where these evolutions are moving is to identify possible convergences. For example, one of the major change phases in the recent evolution of technology has been the practical convergence, or joining together, of the telephone and the computer.

Convergence of evolutions or elements within the evolutions is the real change agent. Anticipating change depends on the convergence of thought patterns and opinions. Much of business success depends upon the convergence of theory and practice.

Challenge

The challenge for business and social organizations is to recognize change as a continuing opportunity, rather than as a threat. In all the areas of evolution and change we have discussed, change creates opportunities for innovative organizations. But change ignored or not anticipated can have a devastating effect. Change is the engine of growth. The key to managing change is in not reacting to change too late (a path that leads to the necessity for revolution). Growth comes from anticipating, adapting to, and generating fresh ideas that exploit the changing conditions. More than ever, an insight into tomorrow is the difference between success and failure.

So how should executives develop the kind of organization that rises to the challenge by being able to anticipate the need for specific changes and is agile enough to see it through? There is no easy or quick answer, though there are many consultants ready to provide "pseudomanagement" remedies. Many of these external messiahs peddle questionable theories and a lot of pretentious psychobabble. Others pour consultants into the company to implement a "learning organization and knowledge-based management." The result of the latter approach in many organizations is the advent of huge IT systems that few use and that actually divert people from a real understanding of the present. The companies who fall for these approaches are also likely to believe that innovation means introducing casual dress days once a week. If this encourages innovation and ease of communication, why on earth restrict it to one day a week? The answer really lies in taking ownership of the need for change, understanding the need for change, and then implementing a *focused* approach relevant to their own culture.

Focus

It is all too easy to proclaim that companies must learn to anticipate change and that management must invest much more in educating and training its people. There is very little talk of how and what the return is, so many do not get engaged in the argument. Others readily accept the theory and are prepared to make the investment. They believe that they have taken ownership of the need, and so there is little point in continuing the debate. They immediately delegate the issue to the HR department and await quick results. A period of change-management seminars and innovation courses makes some interesting waves, but nothing much really changes. There are few simple answers to major business issues. Evolutionary companies have taken time to evolve their approach and their successful cultures. The approach is not easily copied or adopted in a foreign culture to achieve a quick catch-up. The quality revolution and TQM provided ample evidence that adoption is the wrong approach. But the organization that is prepared to take time to first understand the realities of its own culture is soon in a position to *adapt* some of the practices of the evolutionary companies.

The aspiring companies need to *focus* on their own culture, their own customers, their own markets, and their own employees to understand what they need from an investment in *education* and *training*, and above all *management time*. In so doing, they *adapt* an *evolutionary* and *holistic* approach.

Education and Training

The part played by education and training in evolutionary companies is fully developed in Part Three of this book. Executives would also do well to remember that education and training are two different things. Education aims at changing mind-set or the ownership of concepts. Training is the process of learning skills. For example, most parents today would not object to sex education being part of the school curriculum. They might have a very different reaction to sex training! However, there are some elements of the educational process that relate directly to anticipating change; they merit brief mention here.

Apprenticeship

There is no doubt that the practice of apprenticeship (and, in UK terms, the related professional "articled pupil") was tending toward abuse and died as a result. Employers in both manufacturing and service sectors were using the entrants as cheap labor on mundane jobs and not really providing the requisite training. At its best, though, the practice does provide a thorough practical grounding in a particular field. But there have been a number of experiments in subsidized youth training to replace the system. They suffer to some extent from the real intent, as their aim is primarily to reduce the unemployment figures. There is a need to reconsider this whole area of entry to the workplace to establish a fair method of practical training as a basis for a career.

Induction

The evolutionary companies highlighted in this book all take induction to the company very seriously. They provide initial programs that every employee must attend, however well they are qualified. There is strong emphasis on understanding the company's culture and value systems, followed by practical introduction to the various elements of the business. Unfortunately, in the majority of companies this process is at best perfunctory. In too many cases, business school graduates believe that they know it all and end up woefully short of the skills to turn theory into practical action. Induction is another form of apprenticeship when carefully planned and implemented. It is a powerful tool in ensuring continuance of company culture.

Management Development

Many corporations invest heavily in development of their managers, to good effect. However, even the best tend to neglect the educational element of developing a wider perspective and the ability to think outside the box. Focused exercises in observation, upside-down thinking, and purposeful questioning are all elements that do not usually receive sufficient attention.

Knowledge Centers

Several companies have recognized the need for wider and organized dissemination of information throughout the company. As we have seen earlier, this can become a costly IT white elephant, but properly managed it can be a powerful aid in day-to-day action and in anticipating change. Knowledge centers form the centerpiece of what are sometimes called learning organizations; in everyday terms they are really corporate libraries specializing in the company's areas of interest. In many organizations, the person heading this operation is entitled the "knowledge officer" (yes, even called the CKO!). Perhaps it's all a semantic fad, but it is of interest to note that there is only one profession trained to carry out the role intended in this position: the graduate librarian should be eagerly sought after in this arena rather than the computer-literate database manager.

Conclusion

True ability to anticipate and realistically seize opportunities for change relies on the company's ability to develop its people, by constantly seeking answers to the questions: What? Why? When? Where? How? By whom?

But now we need to look a little deeper into some of the major changes happening in the world. The next chapter examines technology change and its impact on business.

Questions for the Reader

1. What effort does your company make to identify areas of change that will affect its future?
2. Have you received any training to help you broaden your perspective?
3. Have you experienced programs designed to make continuous evolutionary change a reality?
4. Do you fear change?
5. Do you feel that the pace of change is continuously moving the goal posts?
6. Do you have any experience or knowledge of the management development practices of the companies named so far in this book?
7. If so, were your reactions to the effort and time expended positive or negative?
8. Have you considered the possible impact of the six evolutions on your working life?

Chapter 7

Whatever Happened to Buck Rogers?

As soon as questions of will or decision or reason or choice of action arise, human science is at a loss.

Noam Chomsky

There are no such things as applied sciences, only applications of science.

Louis Pasteur (1822–1895)

Change is inevitable. In a progressive country change is constant.

Benjamin Disraeli (1804–1881)

If a little knowledge is dangerous, where is the man who has so much as to be out of danger?

T. H. Huxley (1825–1895)

From the early influence of Jules Verne and H. G. Wells, this century has been obsessed with a vision of a future driven by technology. The obsession may have contributed to the collapse of belief that is apparent today, but technology does not stand alone in the evolution of the future. During this century, there have been obvious and dramatic changes brought about by technology, but somehow as we approach the millennium the vision has fallen a little short of expectations. In continuing to look forward to the future impact of technology on our lives, we can learn from the past. The key lessons are as follows:

- The future is never quite as predicted.
- The pace of change is illusory.
- The greatest changes in business come from cost factors and the convergence of distinct technologies.

Fallibility of Prediction

Those who were brought up on the comics of Buck Rogers formed an early impression of the year 2000 that has lived with us ever since. Cities in space were dominated by five-thousand-foot-high futuristic towers with magnetic roadways sweeping around them. Thousands of inhabitants seemed to have their own personal airplanes or were rocketing off for a weekend in space. The comics made for exciting reading and stimulated the imagination. Some of the illustrated predictions have come to pass, but in general the actual millennium is nothing like that—and probably the future never will be. In one of the 1930s comics, Buck is shown in a uniform that is remarkably like those that American astronauts wore when they actually landed on the moon. There was nothing surprising about predicting moon shots; they have dominated science fiction in the past. But Isaac Asimov reminds us that not one science writer had predicted the most remarkable thing about the moon landing: that when it happened the whole world would be watching on television.

Buck Rogers is fiction and designed to entertain rather than to provide accurate predictions of the future. But the predictions of realists or professional soothsayers have proven to be equally fallible. Far from being involved in exciting flights of imagination, they are only trying to make a reasonably accurate forecast of what is going to happen in the future. The further ahead they attempt to forecast, the more astray their predictions are, which talks to the folly of long-term business planning. Three years is long-term.

The magazine *Flying* (now defunct) commissioned a study in 1940 into the future of flying. The resultant report, prepared by responsible members of the aviation industry, noted that the laws of physics provided absolute limits to the performance of "airplanes" of 660 miles per hour at a maximum altitude of 60,000 feet. Less than fifty years later, I flew as an ordinary passenger from London to New York at 1,200 miles per hour at approximately 60,000 feet. To some extent, such predictions were limited by the state of knowledge at the time. But in this particular case, experts in aviation should have known of the existence of jet engines by 1940. At that stage, the existence of the sound barrier (though not recognized by that term) would have been emerging—though, interestingly, the pull of gravity does provide an altitude limitation, without extraordinary power, at about the 60,000 feet level.

The scientist or single-stream technologist can make reasonably accurate predictions for a number of years ahead on physical direction and properties for many distinct technologies. *Unless* a totally new power source is invented, the size, speed, and other performance criteria for automobiles, aircraft, and even computers are relatively easy to predict for the next twenty-five years. But these same people are notoriously bad at predicting what impact those developments will have on the way we work and live. They are also constrained by the perspective of their own discipline.

The recent history of the computer industry provides several examples. The microchip and nonvolatile memory technologies changed possibilities for the computer out of all recognition. They almost removed the problems of energy dispersion (heat) and thus opened the door for miniaturization as well as reducing the crippling cost of memory. One part of the industry stayed in the comfort zone of the familiar and thus predicted that the future needs of their customers would be satisfied by doing the *same* things faster and cheaper. They tended to be those with their hands on the levers of power. Others with a broader perspective saw the developments as an opportunity to do *new* things and open a vast market of *new* customers. Most of the latter could not change the direction of their firms and so left to start up their own businesses.

The leaders of the giant corporations such as IBM and Honeywell predicted the former course. They saw size and price reduction coupled with much-increased transmission speeds as the opportunity for the IT department to distribute the power of the mainframe (and technical control) through "intelligent" terminals. They made a wrong prediction, and within a few years

Honeywell had sold off its computer interests and IBM had terminated sixty thousand people.

For others, it was a new world. Cheap memory and the microchip provided massive opportunity. Cheap miniaturized memory removed most of the constraints on the development of operating and application software, and suddenly it was economically feasible to develop user-friendly software. The microchip allowed a new dimension of processing to be included in a relatively small box not much larger than a terminal. The combination provided those who "saw" with the opportunity to create Microsoft, Apple with its Macintosh, and Compaq. Quite apart from the technical impact, Bill Gates and his compatriots have changed the way we think, work, and live.

New Ways of Working

The computer industry provides many examples of the dangers in long-term prediction of changes to be brought about by technology. They include the "paperless office" and now "the virtual office." They may both happen eventually, but it is far from current experience. Prediction is particularly difficult when it involves integration of several streams of technology and social behavior.

Far from watching the evolution of the paperless office, industry and commerce have been moving in the opposite direction. Other elements in technology have vastly increased the amount of information available to all departments and provided the opportunity to deal with discrete groups of customers and others. Both have multiplied the contact points. The demand for provision of reports, surveys, information, and hard copy for easy transportation have actually resulted in a massive increase in the amount of paperwork being produced and circulated.

However, the very size of the growth may be the spark that starts the evolution, albeit nearly twenty years behind the predictions. From my own observation, companies are wasting a huge amount of time and resources generating, distributing, processing, and storing paperwork that adds no value to the business and actually gets in the way of productive work.

Another prediction arising from the growth of communications technology was that commerce would move rapidly toward the virtual office. It is now possible at reasonable cost to take the office with you: laptop computer, telephone, fax, and printer can be at home or in the car. Soon they will all be enclosed in one container about the size of a briefcase. With this capability, the employee can be working at home or in more regular contact with the customer. The employee is also more likely to be a self-employed "consultant" rather than a salaried worker. It is happening in some service industries but very slowly. Perhaps the reason for the slow movement of this evolution relates more to management practices than to technology. Empowerment and trust are the real keys to this movement; management is reluctant to relinquish command and control.

A simple illustration of moribund management's attitude to technology relates to cellular telephones. When mobile phones first appeared on the general market, they were still expensive. One London consultancy handled that problem by rationing the authority to purchase and have a mobile phone by status. You couldn't have a cell phone unless you were a director. It is the exact opposite of the real value of the mobile telephone. All of those away from the office or on the road were not of sufficient status (forget business need) to have a cellular phone. All of those sitting comfortably in the chateau already in touch with each other had a cell phone. They were extremely useful in improving executive communication with their wives—or mistresses—once they left the office!

Illusory Pace of Change

The pundits are perpetually warning business that the pace of technological change is accelerating and that unless they react immediately they will be left high and dry. As a result, many companies have been stampeded into mindless change. Actually, the time taken for almost every technology to move from introduction to a viable and cost-effective solution to business needs is in reality quite long. It is true that from time to time the opportunity to converge tried-and-tested technologies does speed the process; we touch on that issue later. It is also true that if an organization ignores technological change and continues to operate with its head in the sand, it is asking for trouble.

In the last chapter, we discussed the impact of perspective in viewing change. Let's put the technological and communications "revolution" into perspective. In one breath we are told of the explosion of global business and of vast new markets opening, which can be managed with the information technology and communications technology available on a global basis. But stop for a moment; how widely is this communications technology really available? Have you tried recently to make a cellular phone call from newly technologized countries such as India and China? Or to look at it from another perspective, some two-thirds of all the homes in the world do not have a telephone, and one-half the world's population (about 3 billion people) are still waiting to make their first phone call.

Part of this illusion of the pace of change comes from the mistaken belief being fostered by technical consultants that technology drives modern business. A sense of urgency is being imparted that it would be catastrophic to the business if in any way it were left behind the Joneses. Unless you are in the technology business itself, technology should be viewed only as a tool or enabler to accomplish business objectives. Evolutionary companies are always focused on their customers and their processes. Thus they are continuously considering ways to improve meeting the needs of both. They are rarely rushed by technology; rather, they are pushing the technology suppliers.

A good example comes from Marks and Spencer, one of our featured evolutionary companies. In the 1960s, it was already using bar coding and readers for product identification, stock control, and shelf distribution. Most of their stores had also installed sophisticated electronic cash registers (at least by 1968). We at Honeywell had tried hard to interest them in our "advanced" inventory control processes and other aspects of our product line. Eventually a group of their managers and technical people visited us, and after the introductory pleasantries our team launched into a series of presentations designed to impress M&S. They listened patiently and politely until finally we asked *them* what else they would like to know. They then explained that they knew all about these management systems, and indeed that any major player in the retail and distribution industry who went down the path of our inventory control system would soon be out of business. Now, what they wanted was a technology partner who would design and build a practical and economic way to integrate the technologies of bar codes, image data recognition, and electronic cash registers all linked to a central processor. In other words, the business needs should drive practical application of technology, rather than the other way around. As technologists, we would have considered this an inventory control device because you could use such a system to manage your stocking process. M&S called it a "point of sale" device. Marks and Spencer was not worried about the pace of technology; they were well ahead of the technologists. But the story also underlines the importance of ensuring that the company is thoroughly aware of the trends in technology so that it can innovatively use the benefits for competitive advantage.

Convergence and Cost

With the notable exception of biotechnology, there does not appear to be any major step pending in technology. This is of course a relative term, but in the perspective of their impact on business history the following could be considered major inventions or discoveries:

steam engine
airplane
Bessemer converter
radio
electricity
television
gasoline engine
jet engine
telephone
computer
atomic energy

When considering the pace of invention, it is interesting to note that the last of these major inventions or discoveries dates back into the 1940s. The so-called pace of change relies almost totally on (1) the evolution of the initial invention until it becomes reliable and cost-effective for widespread use and (2) the ability to converge or integrate those inventions.

For example, today the major impact is coming from the convergence of the telephone and the computer, but we have had to wait a long time for this convergence because it would have been pointless unless both had become cost-effective and thus in widespread use. Of course, a host of small inventions are part of the evolution of each invention or discovery.

The opportunities for business from convergence of existing technologies are all around. Such convergence can increase the scope of customer communication, even though some of the devices involved are not perceived as being related to communication, least of all by the customers. In retail outlets, point of sale devices combined with bar coding techniques have helped to develop detailed data on customers, which was one of the objectives for Marks and Spencer back in the 1960s, as we discussed. Such database information allows continuous matching of the broad pattern of customer decisions to goods on the shelf. This use of communication is to the advantage of both parties.

The British supermarket chain Tesco has now taken this concept into new realms with the launch of its Clubcard. Tesco has converged two familiar and well-proven technologies, the point of sale device with the credit card, for a different purpose. The linkage between the technologies already exists for those customers who wish to pay via credit card. The Clubcard is a loyalty or discount card rather than a credit card, but applicants for "membership in the club" are happy to provide substantial personal information on their application form. The converged technology enables Tesco to *personalize* nearly every sale and extend its database. In only six weeks, Tesco built up more than five million detailed personal records of *individual* customer decisions. Individual customer preferences or buying patterns can be tracked and identified across the whole range of products, store by store.

As a result, customers can be invited to special events or be offered special opportunities that are directly related to their preferences. Even "lost" customers can be identified and strategies devised to entice them back. One of the world's largest supermarket chains is now able to act like a local shopkeeper who "knows" the customer. This capability has had a major impact on business performance, but it would have been deemed impossible only a few years ago.

The real point of the story is that the technologies involved were well tried and tested and had been used economically by Tesco *and their competitors* for a long time. In fact, some of their competitors viewed the loyalty card as a sales gimmick similar to Green Stamps. They have since followed Tesco's lead. It was innovative business thinking, not technology, that made the breakthrough.

Attitude and Comprehension

There is nothing to fear from technological change for business if it creates an attitude of curiosity, innovation, and confidence in its people to challenge conventional wisdom. That does not mean that every individual in the organization is a creator or a technology buff. However, they recognize, and are a committed part of, a culture that welcomes risk taking. This is mainly an attitude that encourages people to step outside the box and look at the business with a new perspective. In a wider context, there are problems associated with working outside the box, which we touch on later.

In reality, the more common attitude to recognizing customer needs is centered within the narrow focus of its own technology. Another example from the computer industry illustrates the closed mind of so many technologists. In the late 1960s, the computer industry began to dabble in the management sciences and so-called management information systems. This whole period in the industry is interesting in retrospect and also fairly typical of the evolution of new products. Many of us involved in the industry at the time were enthusiastically committed to it and arrogantly believed that we were in the best position to advise our customers how to reorganize their businesses in the new computer age. With ease, we moved outside our core competencies. This is still typical of the thought processes in many "high-tech" companies and consultancies.

A somewhat amusing experience of my own illustrates this attitude of closed perspective. In the early 1970s, I was manager of industry marketing at Honeywell at the forefront of this arrogant nonsense. The management sciences team was developing "customer presentations" on their packages designed to solve business problems and now wanted agreement from me on their marketing approach. To my amazement, their presentation used as references to the success of their concepts the TSR II military aircraft project, the construction of the *QE2*, and the Concorde project. All of these projects were famed in Britain as total management failures in their late delivery and massive cost overruns. I queried their enthusiasm for these examples. The reply was breathtaking in its ignorance of the market: "That may be true, but you don't really understand the technology. These are perfect examples of implementing PERT and critical path analysis." They were shocked when I sent them packing and told them to think again. But their attitudes are typical of many technocrats working secure in a little world of their own making.

Forecasts for the Future

So what's coming next? I am not qualified to make such predictions, but three recent reports based on the research of technology crystal-gazers provide some intriguing insight. They could stimulate some innovative business thinking.

British Telecommunications (BT) set up a team, led by Ian Pearson, to predict the shape of things to come in the next century. It says that within twenty years cancer will be preventable, space tours will have begun, online voting in elections will be operational, and the petabit (one million trillion, in American figures) memory chip will have arrived. The BT team has come to its conclusions by talking to experts in key fields and combing research papers. The findings have been incorporated in a calendar, to provide three dates for each development: the first likely, the most likely, and the latest possible dates. The calendar covers medicine, biotechnology, energy, business, education, machines, information technology, man-machine interfaces, materials, memory and storage, robotics, security, space, transport, and of course telecommunications. The calendar can be accessed on the Internet to alert individuals and institutions to developments

that affect their activities. (The Internet address is http:
//www.labs.bt.com/people/pearsonid/.)

Pearson says that a prediction that by 2020 the average life
span will be one hundred years is primarily based on the medical
advances that will have occurred over the previous twenty-three
years, including artificial pancreas (by 1998), personal wearable
health monitors (2005), artificial heart (2010), prevention of cancer (2013), artificial lungs and kidney (2015), and artificial liver
(2020). Young people will have a longer life span, and if these
developments continue the life span could eventually go up to
140. Virtual-reality exercises will be in use by 1998–99 to improve health, and the whole human DNA sequence will have
been determined by 2005. Ten years from then, the genetic links
of all diseases will have been identified and the individual's genome (the complete set of genes) will become part of the medical card.

Computers that write their own software will be around in
2005, and neurocomputers, based on the human brain, will have
been developed by 2016. The calendar predicts that small domestic robots will be in by 2005, with the first—a robotic lawn
trimmer—out in 1997. More than thirty other predictions are
made for robotics, ranging from totally automated factories
(2007) to robotic exercise companions (2020) and house-trained
robots doing the domestic chores. On technology for space, the
calendar predicts near-earth space tours by 2015 and regular
manned missiles to Mars by 2026. For long journeys in space,
human hibernation will have been developed by 2030. In telecommunications, the wrist phone should be available (by now)
and the hand videophone by 2000, the same year that speech
dialing is predicted. Full-voice interaction with machines will be
available in 2005.

Although most of the events predicted are beneficial, the
calendar warns of the possibility of disasters that could happen
at any time, given the appropriate circumstances. These wild-
card events, predicted for BT by John Petersen of the Arlington
Institute in Virginia, include a virus becoming immune to all
known treatments; long-term side effects of a common medica-
tion could be revealed; ice caps could break up and cause ocean
levels to rise 100 feet; and human mutation, collapse of the
sperm count, and terrorist use of biological weapons.

The international technology magazine *Wired* conducted a

survey of scientific futurologists, which it published in December 1996. It includes many of the same predictions as in the BT report (though not always the same dates) but adds interesting detail in some more prosaic areas that are just as likely to affect our lives. At the turn of the century it will be possible to buy custom-designed clothes that are measured by digital body-scanners and delivered to shoppers within twenty-four hours (author's note: I have been able to do that in Bombay or Hong Kong for a number of years!). Custom-tailored clothes for the masses at reasonable prices by 1999 will have a massive impact on all elements of the clothing industry. Within a further ten years, clothes will be made of "smart" fabrics that can alter their properties to keep people warm in winter and cool in summer. The scientists say that eventually fabrics will have embedded electronics to enable our clothes to serve as computer screens or communication devices.

Nanotechnology, which operates at a scale of one billionth of a meter, will produce a wealth of new devices for the home. Microscopic robots will remove rust and reconfigure plastic. A toilet seat that changes shape for whoever sits on it will become a reality. The *Wired* survey predicts that robots capable of cleaning houses will be in the stores within ten years. Some scientists envisage small armies of robotic "cockroaches" emitting static charges that would act as magnets for dust.

Medicine will gain most from nanotechnology, says professor Richard Smalley of Rice University in Texas. Doctors will use a tiny biological sensor on the tip of a needle, which will be able to tell instantly which chemicals are present in a patient's blood. By 2010, robots and nanotechnology will be combined in a single pill-sized device that can be sent into the body to perform delicate surgical tasks, for example patching stomach ulcers or removing polyps in the bowel.

Combined evolutions in drug design will produce fat-destroying pills. By 2015, experts believe, all the daily dietary requirements of a human being will be available in a pill the size of an aspirin. By 2020 a reliable "sober-up" pill will be available.

Our final source, *Business Week,* produced a special report entitled "The Biotech Century" in March 1997. Again, the publishers sought the views of leading biotechnologists. Nobel prize-winning chemist Robert Curl of Rice University said that "This was the century of physics and chemistry, but it is clear that the next century will be the century of biology." The report high-lighted a road map for biotech research that was allowing scientists to get at the most basic functions of life, deep inside the complex interactions of genes. Here are some of the mind-bog-gling developments on the road map:

- Hemophilus: This bacterium, which causes meningitis and childhood ear infections, was the first organism for which researchers identified the entire genome. This has opened the door to new drugs and vaccines.
- Cloning: Dr. Ian Wilmut and his colleagues added new genes to 277 eggs before they got one to grow into Dolly, the world's most famous sheep. New researchers are rushing to duplicate the feat with other animals. The possibility of human cloning has raised a major moral debate. It could provide the technological answer to man's desire for immortality: as the existing body wears out, the individual could arrange for her or his own cloning.
- Family trees: Researchers are now using large families, often from genetically isolated communities, together with powerful computer technology to identify genes involved in complex disorders such as diabetes and heart disease.
- Mustard weed: Researchers have begun to decipher the complete genome of this plant. The eventual result could be supercrops or trees that would yield such products as plastics and drugs. (This particular development reminds me of the famous BBC TV April Fools' joke that fooled millions. An otherwise-serious weekly documentary program featured a disturbing blight that was affecting spaghetti trees and worried about its possible impact on the Italian diet.)
- DNA chips: The convergence of microchips and DNA are a natural. Researchers are using chips to rapidly identify genetic variations in specific tissues. Being able to compare diseased and healthy tissue can reveal causes of disease.
- Yeast, drosophila, *C. elegant*: Two of these organisms—fruit flies and tiny worms—are very close to being sequenced; yeast has already been done. Many of their

genes are remarkably similar to human genes, which offers new clues to eliminate diseases such as malaria.

Conclusion

It is very clear that the evolution of change brought about by technology is continuing and will make dramatic changes in our life. Looking at some of the predictions, we see that it would appear that the greatest impact will come from the convergence of information technology and biotechnology. However, what is obvious is that the direction of the varying facets of research are clear and available to those who are interested. Perhaps most important from the business perspective is that each facet takes a considerable time and investment to evolve into cost-effective applications. The evolutionary company that continuously monitors developments in technology and customer needs is not caught out by the pace of these changes.

Questions for the Reader

1. In your organization, are managers regularly briefed on developments in technology?
2. To what degree is innovation fostered in your organization?
3. What change in technology has made the biggest impact on your business?
4. Had that specific technology been known about and used by your competitors before you?
5. Has your company organized forums of your customers to consider the direction their businesses are going, in order to help you interpret their future needs?
6. Have you seen examples of introducing technology without developing company culture, procedures, etc., to take best advantage of the change?
7. What would be the impact on worldwide capital investment if there were another massive Tokyo earthquake?
8. What is likely to change in your organization if the average life expectancy is one hundred years by 2020?

Chapter 8

A Global Challenge

"If everyone minded their own business," said the Duchess in
a hoarse growl, "the world would go round a deal faster than
it does."

Alice in Wonderland, Lewis Carroll (1832–1898)

Forward let us range,
Let the great world spin forever down the ringing grooves of change.

Alfred, Lord Tennyson (1809–1892)

The greatest change for business is the emergence of a truly
global economy. Today, this evolving economy is dominated by
well-known multinational corporations, which account for a
growing share of global products and services. These global players no longer come automatically from the United States or the
European Economic Union. A particular facet of the change over
recent decades had been the emergence in different industries
and services of new giants from Japan, Korea, Singapore, Malay-
sia, and Taiwan.

The collapse of the Soviet Union and the resulting movement toward "liberalization" across vast areas of the world such
as Eastern Europe, Russia, India, to some extent China, and
South America has opened the doors of international trade and
thus hastened the evolution of the global economy.

Would-be players in the wider economy are going to have to
learn that there is a big difference between the traditional international company selling around the world with satellite operations in many countries and the one that is a totally global

enterprise. The role of the multinational changes dramatically in attitudes to competition, to partnership with local communities, and in fundamental cultures. In aiming to be big, they first have to learn to be small.

But a word of warning. The evolution toward global economy is once again not at such a pace that there is a need for panic reaction and mindless change. Heed the advice of Sir Richard Greenbury, chairman of Marks and Spencer: "I am a tortoise, and Marks and Spencer is a tortoise, and we don't do things until we have thought them through very carefully."

Global Patterns

The growth of the global economy stems from a number of factors such as the free flow of capital, technological change, sociopolitical change, and innovations in business attitudes. The evolution has been speeded by penetration of market-based concepts into countries that were formally bastions of protectionism and bureaucratic control.

For much of the postwar period, more than three-quarters of the world's people lived in countries whose governments were skeptical of, or openly hostile to, the concept of free markets or indeed any form of international communication for their people. Since 1990, this has changed dramatically. The developing countries have vastly increased their share of world manufacturers and their GDP has grown and brought them a substantial rise in consumption and imports. They are rapidly helping to shape the global economy.

The sheer size of the markets and the wealth of the United States, Europe, and Japan means that most of their corporations will for some time continue to operate predominantly in large established markets. But leading evolutionary companies are busy establishing alliances and working at opening opportunities in the new markets of South East Asia, South America, and Eastern Europe. There is mounting evidence that these markets will continue to grow at an even faster rate.

The process is helped because increasingly governments are recognizing that their home prosperity depends on the activities of foreign international companies. As a result, they have begun to remove barriers and collaborate with bodies such as the World Trade Organization and other governments. India and others have joined GATT (General Agreement on Tariffs and Trade) and entered into agreements that include acceptance of concepts such as copyright and that protect products from copying and the stealing of intellectual rights. For many companies, particularly in the financial sector, national boundaries are disappearing.

However, this movement to liberalization is not universally accepted. Amazingly, resistance is most common in the nations that have most to gain from the global economy in the long run. Old established industries can see the global market as a threat rather than as an opportunity. They feed on the anxieties of areas of potential unemployment and the general reaction of society to major change. Unfortunately, they command formidable lobbying power, which inhibits government. In a similar manner, others use economic nationalism to restrict competition and collaboration between nation states. Europe and the United States in their different ways both exhibit these reactions to the global economy.

Protectionism does not create growth or jobs. Trade with the developing world has created virtually every new job in Europe during the last ten years. Jobs based on exports tend to be higher-paying jobs because they rely on higher skills. France and to a lesser extent Germany are seeking to protect lower-paid jobs in competing sectors (such as agriculture and public services) at the expense of higher-paying jobs in the export market. It is a prescription for economic decline.

The drivers on which national growth and wealth were based are also changing. At one time fertile land, temperate climate, natural resources, and capital were the arbiters of economic success. Modern food technology has destroyed the Malthusian fears; capital is readily available from the international finance markets; and natural resources, with the possible exception of the Middle East, do not seem to determine national success. Now technological prowess, innovative products, and intellectual property are the keys to opening global markets.

In the face of the global economy, national governments have less room for maneuvering and are steadily becoming less powerful. As for business corporations, more alliances are necessary, which means that power is passed to supranational organizations such as the European Union or is shared in bodies such as NATO, NAFTA (the North American Free Trade Agreement), or GATT. All are restrictions on the traditional power of national governments. In addition, technology has enabled the free flow of money and information to the extent that policy of national governments has little influence on the value of currencies, the level of interest rates, or the freedom of national governments to ensure that multinational corporations contribute to tax revenues. More often, governments are enticing multinationals to operate in their environment by providing tax concessions.

As the walls have come tumbling down and nations are tentatively walking in the new global environment, new concerns have arisen. From a business perspective, trade and products need to be protected; from a social point of view, people and the environment have rights to be preserved; and from an international perspective, the terms of engagement have to be agreed. All of this has led to a series of regulatory bodies and a host of regulations and risks that are becoming increasingly difficult to manage or even understand. In the West and in particular in the United States, the reaction has seen the growth of nonproductive activities that in some fields are already crippling competitiveness. Hamish McRae, in his interesting book *The World in 2020*, notes two of these activities. The first is the legal profession. Around three-quarters of the world's lawyers live in the United States. In 1960, in the United States there were 260,000 lawyers; in 1990 there were 756,000. In comparison, Japan, with one-half the population of the United States, manages with fewer than 15,000 lawyers. It is a dubious statistic, but it would seem that the number of lawyers in a country is in direct proportion to its growth rate. It is not just the ludicrous fees that businesses (and individuals) pay to lawyers but the inhibiting effect that they have on so much decision making that is the real danger.

Another area of inhibiting overhead to American and European decision making noted by McRae is the growth in political lobbying. In 1956, there were 4,900 trade associations fighting for specialized corners; this had risen in the United Kingdom to 23,000 by 1989. The number of political lobbyists registered with the U.S. Senate was 360 in 1960; that rose to 40,111 in 1992. But the same is happening in Brussels as new regulations flow from the European Commissioners. Of course, the principal reason for the growth of these activities is the rise in regulation. Both the United States and British governments have made electoral play of deregulation and making government "simple." But in a complex world, this appears very difficult to achieve.

In this overview of global patterns, John Naisbitt makes an interesting point in *Global Paradox* that as a contributor to the global economy, tourism has no equal. Consider the following:

- Tourism employs 204 million people worldwide, or 10.6 percent of the global workforce.
- Tourism is the world's leading contributor, producing 10.2 percent of the world gross national product.
- Tourism is the world's largest industry in terms of gross output, approaching $3.4 trillion.

In addition, it is worth noting that an increasing percentage of tourism is to the more unusual, exotic or remote parts of the world. Quite apart from business taking part in the global economy, a vast number of people in the world are voting with their sandals for a broader perspective. This movement in itself gradually changes social and business perspectives.

An interesting perspective on this increasing globalization can be gained from the observation of the major management consultancies. They not only have to be big but also have to operate globally. The world's most successful companies (the consultants' clients) operate globally and expect their consultancies to do the same. They want consultant companies to provide seamless service across borders and personnel who can handle international mergers, alliances, or acquisitions. A global presence is also an important element in recruiting the very best graduates.

In response to these pressures, consultancies are now expanding abroad. Some are buying local companies while others are trying to meld their existing collection of offices into a global network. Firms that previously were dominated by a single culture (usually American) are becoming multicultural. For example, three of the most venerable American firms, McKinsey, Bain, and Booz-Allen, are now headed by non-Americans (respectively, an Indian, an Israeli, and an Irishman). All have found that globalization is fraught with problems. The most obvious is that establishing an intangible product in a new marketplace takes time and patience. Many smaller consultancies have withdrawn after years of frustration and loss. Another problem is recruitment and retention of staff, particularly in the fast-developing economies of Asia. Well-qualified people are at a premium for growing local industries, making them harder to keep. The fundamental issue for most consultancies is whether to grow organically or by acquisition. The former provides cultural continuity but can be very slow. A growing number of companies are choosing growth by acquisition. This approach also has its risks, but that is what business judgment is all about.

Competition

The global economy is not for the fainthearted or the incompetent. There are hungry sharks out there, and the competition is fierce. There are no local governments to protect individual companies. National economies are increasingly affected by the result of decisions by major multinationals. True competitiveness in a global environment is determined by corporations, not national governments. The new leaders are those corporations that can steadily build market share, whether they are producing and selling in competitive or noncompetitive areas. The competitive economies are those receiving the profits of those giants.

The ability to compete effectively in such widespread markets depends on the exportability of core competencies. Dependent upon the industry in which they operate, this can be a difficult test for even the biggest corporations. As a result, a series of mergers or strategic alliances—often between erstwhile competitors—are taking place, enabling the new group to compete across the board. Corporations need to be certain that they are fit to compete. But this does not mean that only giant corporations are suited to the global economy.

Small Is Big

There are a number of reasons why the global economy provides opportunities for the small or medium-sized company:

- As in nature, great corporate sharks need parasites to provide a host of specialized services. Of course, the majority are found in specific operational areas, but as we noted with consultancies high technical knowledge or competency follows the big corporations.
- Giant organizations are themselves breaking down their bureaucratic organizations into confederations of small entrepreneurial companies. They tend to form partnerships with other small entrepreneurial groups with specialized knowledge.
- The latest technology is now cheap enough to be available for the small company, which gives it great mobility.
- Deregulation and globalization of financial markets have given relatively small companies access to investment capital once denied to them.
- Since liberalization, it is much easier for the small company to gain access to new markets without the massive costs of legal support (and in many cases bribery).
- Bright entrepreneurial people no longer automatically seek the large corporation. They want more responsibility and challenge at a much earlier age. They are attracted to the small company, or they group together to set up their own.

Jack Welch, the legendary CEO of GE, says "Think small." He adds, "What are we trying relentlessly to do is to get that small-company soul—and small-company speed—inside our big company body." He explains further, "We are trying to get the small-company benefits of quickness in time to market, decision making, and the elimination of bureaucratic activities."

A New Role

Historically, individuals and organizations have naturally become linked to and identified with their place of origin. In the initial stage of the global evolution, that identity can be to the advantage of the external corporation. But the level of mobility is having an impact on the personnel of both the multinational corporation and the local business. The world is steadily becoming much less place-related. This is changing the involvement of corporate responsibility. In the initial phases, business people have learned to become chameleons in their perceived involvement in the areas in which they operate.

An Arthur Andersen partner shared the firm's attitude with me: "For the majority of our existence we have had to defend our position as the 'Chicago' accountants—now we are having to overcome the label of the 'American' accountants." The global multinationals have to adapt to, and to some extent become part of, the local cultures in which they operate. But identity and involvement with local problems and positive involvement can encourage movement toward reliance. A new alternative religion is being created as the focus of life shifts to the corporate giant.

The major corporations that have made a strategic decision to grow in the global market place are consciously changing their overseas culture and working policies. Modern communication and all-pervasive media mean that there are no remote places left. A company that mistreats or exploits its workers (and animals) soon has a protest group condemning its every movement. But many are now changing for positive reasons. They are acting as responsible members of the community. In many areas of the world, they are acting a little like the great Quaker manufacturers of the last century. Highly developed cultures would see some of these policies as patronizing; to an extent they are, but they are also improving living standards, health, home hygiene, educational standards, and the general quality of life for millions. The corporation is increasingly taking over the role of government in many areas.

In many ways, the vast multinational corporation is well suited to take over international leadership of society. Consider some of its advantages:

- It is temporal and concerned with reward in the relatively short term.
- It has command of a congregation through its employment policies.
- It generally has the funds.
- It has the power structure both in relation to its own management and in alliances with other sociopolitical groups in the countries in which it trades.

⦿ It is involved in education and training, and in some areas it is already the sought-after alternative to the state educational system.

The Changing Globe

Businesspeople are not unaware of politics or geopolitical issues in general. International market opportunities and self-interest alone stimulate interest in what is happening in the wider world. But whatever the motivation, many companies do take a keen interest in world affairs and often employ advisors and consultants to keep them briefed on specific areas. Perhaps naturally there is a tendency to concentrate their attention on the immediate issues for their particular business. The mass of detail involved in the political minutiae of international business, from customs duties and currency rates to a host of regulatory restraints, tends to obscure the essential broader trends going on around them. Evolutionary companies are more likely to view the world with a broader perspective. This is partly because they have made a conscious decision to do so, but it also happens naturally because of the culture of the organization. They are continuously asking questions.

Economic Outlook

The collapse of Russian Communism has made it self-evident that market-led economies work better than centrally planned economies. If ever proof was needed, the comparison between West Germany and East Germany, where the same people prospered under one system but regressed under the other, was the nearest thing to a controlled experiment that exists in economic research. In making the same point in an article in the *London Sunday Times*, Andrew Neil has said that there are three distinct economic models evolving in the market economy; he defines these as the Asian, the European, and the American model.

The Asian model involves small government with close links to business, low taxes, minimal welfare, high savings to finance investment, and strong families to ensure social discipline. The European social democratic model has produced big government, high taxes, rigid labor markets, and lavish social welfare. The American free-market model works with moderate government, taxes, and welfare; and flexible labor markets. The British economy is in transition, but with the election of Tony Blair it continues to move strongly toward the American model.

Of course, the perspective of time and place does not provide an easy solution for world nations at different stages of development. For example, the Asian model is not a realistic objective for mature industrial economies. It works best for developing nations with authoritarian governments enforcing economic discipline and social cohesion. There is evidence that the successful Asian economies, such as those of Japan, South Korea, and Taiwan, are encountering difficulties in this model as affluence makes them more democratic.

The central European model provides little to teach the world; it is moribund. As Neil notes, it has "ceased to work; it no longer provides jobs for its people." The jobless rate in Japan is currently only 3.5 percent, in America it is 5.5 percent, and the UK has 7 percent; but in Germany it is 15 percent and in France 20 percent in many areas. In addition, Europe spends billions in extensive employment and make-work subsidies. Europe can change, but it requires leaders of courage, and time is running out. Prior to 1979, the United Kingdom was languishing far behind its European partners, but Margaret Thatcher has changed all that. These disparate performances within Europe and international comparisons are important outside the economic sphere. They are creating strains within Europe as the process of union advances toward a single currency. A great international experiment is encountering stormy seas in which the whole concept may founder unless Central Europe wakes up to a real understanding of a market-led economy.

The free-market American model is a huge job-creating machine. In the last twenty-five years, despite the massive impact of global competition, the American economy has generated forty-six million extra jobs, while Europe has struggled to a few million and is now actually falling back. America has many problems, but creating jobs is not one of them. It would also be wrong to assume that these jobs were all in low-paid service areas or part-time. The U.S. Council of Advisors has reported that 70 percent of the new jobs are in high-wage occupations, including 60 percent in the professional or managerial capacity. The world's richest country is still full of vigor.

National Perspectives

Before moving to some of the wider implications of the geopolitical movements in the world, we should consider some of the national changes and perspectives likely to influence the whole. The key areas are as follows:

> The United States
> Russia and its dependents
> Japan
> Emerging giants: China and India
> Europe

An immediate reaction to this list is that it excludes more than one-third of the world's nations and geographic areas with the omission of Africa, South America, and Australasia. But at this stage of history they are being influenced by events rather than influencing them.

The United States

Since the middle of World War II, the United States has been the wealthiest and most powerful nation on earth. With the collapse of Russia, this position has become indisputable. The achievement of America has been immense, from its early days as the dream "mother of liberty" to its success as a superpower. It accomplished the victory in World War II and contributed magnificently with the Marshall Plan to aid reconstruction after the war. As a nation, the United States has been the most munificent great power in history, and its people are legend for their hospitality to visitors.

Despite its responsible approach to power, the United States has been reviled around the world. It is considered naïve and totally insensitive to other cultures and the aspirations of other nations. From some perspectives, it is portrayed as a nation racked by interracial hostility and ridden by violent crime. Of course, a great deal of this criticism is steeped in envy of the rich neighbor, particularly from some of the former great powers. Some of it is just sheer nonsense based on ignorance. But there is an underlying sense that the United States has somehow squandered the American dream. There are two elements to this perception, namely, (1) United States citizens are no longer interested in the American Dream, and (2) the United States has lost interest in a world role.

From the latter part of the last century, the United States took pride in the fact that it was able to take people from all countries, races, and religions and make them into good Americans. Many of them retained a sentimental attachment to the place of their birth, but all immigrant groups became Americans first. They were Irish-Americans, Italian-Americans, or Jewish-Americans on a secondary level. As recently as the 1960s, new immigrants were regarded as working hard and willingly to learn about the constitution and to master sufficient English to earn the right to become an American citizen. To them, citizenship was an achievement and a matter of great pride. This was the American Dream, the great melting pot which was able to turn all these different people into a single nation.

Somehow, this great strength of the United States appears to have been lost, or at least is in decline. I can remember my own sense of shock when visiting Miami to find that so many of the signs at the airport and in public buildings were in Spanish. It was all being done with the best intentions, but I believe it was the outward sign that the United States appears to be a nation divided in itself (what was the Civil War about?). A nation in which blacks are hostile to Asians, who in turn are hostile to Hispanics, and all are hostile to whites. Now the citizen is an African-American or Hispanic-American first and a simple American second. Some of this tendency is fostered by the cult of political correctness, which is closing the liberal mind of America. From the perspective of the outside world, this evolution is damaging America's emotional and spiritual right to lead a new democratic world.

Since the end of the Gulf War, the U.S. government and the

people of America seem to have lost interest in the world. Throughout the Cold War, there was a national commitment, backed by public opinion, to take on the role of the guardian of world order. Now when it is needed so desperately, that commitment is lacking and the United States has entered a period of tacit isolationism. The United States does not appear to have clear international objectives or policies to support a world role, and any international policies that emerge from time to time are chiefly concerned with domestic electoral impact; hence the window-dressing policies, we British conclude, regarding the Irish Republican Army. Hopefully this is but a passing phase. The world needs American leadership, even if only as a policeman.

Russia and Its Dependents

The West's response to its defeat of the Soviet Union has been less responsible than that toward its earlier defeated enemies Germany and Japan. Of course, the circumstances were entirely different. The collapse came from economic rather than military war and thus came from within. Also, the victorious Western alliance didn't occupy the territories of its former enemy. But at the end of the earlier conflict, a responsible and generous America realized that future world peace would not be achieved by economic destruction of such major powers. The Marshall Plan was an imaginative approach to building a new economic structure from reconstruction. Nothing remotely similar came from the Western alliance in the years following 1991. Indeed, the West went further in the other direction by ensuring that all aid was directly linked to introduction of political and economic reforms designed to replace the existing system with a free-market economy system. The West is flirting with anarchy; a very dangerous affair.

In our eagerness to convert the heathen, we seemed to forget that Russia and the new nations of Belarus, Moldavia, and the Ukraine had no knowledge or experience of what was involved in a democratic system or a free-market economy. My own understanding of what this really meant started when I read a report that a major Japanese company was withdrawing any trading in Russia because it found it impossible to get payment. This surprised me because my own experience of dealing with

Russia and Eastern Europe in the 1970s was so different. It was certainly an arduous task to negotiate a deal, but once concluded, communist countries met every deadline in the agreement (even though it was sometimes at five minutes before midnight on the last day). It had nothing to do with honesty, but the slow grinding wheels of bureaucracy. It is of interest that the same bureaucratic culture delivered vital raw materials to Germany on the night that Hitler launched Barbarossa. It is the way the *system* works.

On investigation, the answer was illuminating. The industrial complex involved had never received an "invoice" before, and it just didn't know how to handle it. In the comfortable communist past, all such matters were handled by a centralized purchasing and payment agency. In the sophisticated economies of the West, when we talk about the need for an improved infrastructure we tend to visualize new highways, railroad connections, or local airports. That is not really the first problem for Russia. Consider the problems confronting a would-be entrepreneur in Russia or East Europe. Under the new laws, he or she now has complete freedom to set up his or her own business. What is needed now is some land, to construct an office and a factory, some vehicles to distribute the product, and an opportunity to communicate with prospective customers. Reasonable; but how on earth do you accomplish that in a Russian town? There are no realtors to help you find the land, there are no private architects or construction companies to build your facilities, there is no advertising access to newspapers or the television, and no one can rely on the postal or telephone service. There is no Hertz or Avis or any other like agency to rent or lease cars or trucks. Finally, there are no local lawyers or bankers (or even a bank) to provide essential business services. Too few lawyers and bankers may seem like heaven to Western businesspeople, but in reality we do need *some* of them (a great new opportunity for lend-lease!). In essence, we have pushed Russia too fast to move to a market-based economy. As a result, a new Mafia has filled the middle ground, extracting exorbitant fees or protection monies and bribing an unpaid military to deliver some of the missing services. Corruption and crime are destroying the opportunity to create a new free-market area and early welcoming of democracy. Across Eastern Europe and the old nations of the Soviet Union, former communists are once again being elected as cynicism grows.

With this background, it is highly unlikely that Russia and its dependents will rapidly become modern democracies on the Western model. From an economic point of view, there is no need for them to do so. The major economies have had no problem in the past in dealing with successful economic countries with little or no democratic tradition. The practical questions are whether all these former members of the Soviet Union can live peacefully with each other. The West should try to find out what help they need to provide a practical infrastructure and cope with their environmental problems. Solve these issues, and they will start to contribute to the World economy.

One noted commentator on the state of Russia, David Remnick, in his latest book *The Struggle for a New Russia*, states that "The Russian prospect over the coming years and decades is more promising than ever before in its history." He goes on to say, "Russia has entered the world, and everything, even freedom, even happiness, is now possible."* I would not go that far, but I do believe that we are being overly negative in our assessment of the future Russian contribution. The technical skills of Russia remain as strong as ever, and the educated human resource is enormous. Russia also controls massive resources of raw materials, including natural gas, that are already playing a part in the economics of Western Europe. There are huge markets available to Russia and the former members of the Soviet Union. If the West can help this area create a climate of political stability and support modernization of its infrastructure massive, private investment will be available from both Europe and Japan.

Japan

There is also instability in Japanese politics. For decades, Japan has been ruled by stable right-wing governments of the Liberal Democratic Party. The LDP has been plagued by corruption, and its continued election was hardly an advertisement for Japanese democracy, but it worked for Japan. Now, following a series of scandals, there is an uncomfortable coalition of the Left and the

*New York: Random House, 1997.

Right that is proving ineffective in dealing with the economic crisis. This period of boom and bust will come to an end, but Japan's vaunted expertise will never seem quite the same.

Emerging Giants: China and India

China and India will be competing for the title of the world's greatest economic power within fifty years. Both have advantages and disadvantages. China has been there before. Less than two hundred years ago, China could claim to be the world's biggest power and greatest civilization. India has long been a great civilization, but internal divisions and a fatalistic subservience have prevented it from becoming a great power to date.

Both nations are nuclear powers, which is what used to define superpower status. India has not been tempted to become a major military power but was instead content to rely on the Western umbrella during the Cold War. China, on the contrary, has grown its military might, believing that it was in military competition with both the Soviet Union and the United States. The Chinese economic expansion of the last decade has been faster than India's, but the subcontinent is rapidly catching up. In a similar fashion, China has the larger population, but India's is growing, and if the birth rate continues at the same pace India will overtake China by approximately 2020. Each country will have a population close to 1.5 billion within the next fifty years. At that stage, the United States will have a population of close to 300 million. There is a dangerous assumption in the West that these vast millions are going to be ill-educated peasants who create a drain on a modern economy. It is true that millions do live in poverty, but the investment in education in both countries is massive. Their current involvement in high-tech industries and software development is evidence of the quality of labor in both countries. To spend time in both countries is only to underline the immense thirst for education their people have.

As the largest democracy in the world, India is in a better political position to adapt to the market-led economy. However, it shares with China a massive and corrupt bureaucracy that inhibits much of their people's natural entrepreneurship. Recently in India I watched the Republic Day parade in New Delhi on television. I was amused to hear the TV commentator refer to the main viewing stand as being reserved for VIPs "and other bureaucrats"! One of the few countries in the world where the term *bureaucrat* is one of approbation rather than opprobrium.

There are some worries that could impede the growth of both and also pose some threats for future world peace. They are subject to the movements or evolutions we touch on later in this chapter, namely the ethnic issues, the rise of nationalism, tribalism, and the collapse of accepted faiths. The most worrying factor is the rather nasty nationalistic habit that China has picked up in recent decades. The whole pace of change within China creates problems for her political leaders. Currently, the leaders of China appear weak and may fall for the temptation of all weak governments to seize a moment for aggressive action to prove their virility. The recent return to Hong Kong may also stimulate their appetite. Such opportunities could become available on the Tibetan borders, the long borders with the old Soviet Union, and perhaps most important the tempting morsel of the twenty-one million highly productive people of Taiwan. Over the next few years, America may need to tame the "Beijing Dragon" to preserve world peace.

Europe

The countries that make up what is called continental Europe and to a lesser extent the United Kingdom have allowed themselves to become obsessed with the objective of rapid evolution of the European Union to the exclusion of other world issues. A new Bismarck in the fitting shape of Chancellor Helmut Kohl is attempting to unite the States of Europe into a new single currency and federal state, with Germany as its political center. Before this sounds like prejudice, I must state that I am idealistically drawn to a United Europe (in the 1960s I was a representative to the Council of Europe in Strasbourg). However, I have never expected a thousand years of nationalistic history to be changed overnight. To my mind, the first priority is to enlarge the concept and to ensure that the community embraces the eastern states that were formerly subjugated into the Soviet Empire, before rushing to the federal state.

Europe, more than the rest of the world, still has to fully adjust to the fall of the Soviet Empire. Tensions that have been suppressed for at least two generations will not disappear at the behest of a European commissioner based in Brussels. But Europe was the cradle of Western civilization and economic power. It would be very unwise to write off the possibility of a united, greater Europe competing with the other emerging world giants over the next fifty years.

Nationalism and Tribalism

Nationalism and tribalism are very different but are often confused in forecasting trends of the future. It is certainly confusing the arguments in Europe over steady evolution toward federalism. Nationalism in the sense of the nation state is dated and on the decline. No doubt as unionism grows there will be an element of nostalgia, and people will hold on to many national attitudes and traditions—a little like the American Irish. In a sense, America could be seen as starting this evolution; it is a union of many states combining a mongrel mix of many nationalities. Already, it has started the process of extending the union with development of the North American Free Trade Area. Tribalism, on the other hand, is on the increase within many areas and has some very dangerous elements such as fundamentalism and terrorism.

The nation state is under attack from a number of influences, both internal and external. Internal pressures arise from minority groups within the state, both ethnic and religious, which are finding their own allegiances outside the state. Growing uncertainty and insecurity, perhaps derived from a sense of not belonging, are creating undertones that include racial tension. The external influences are rapidly making the nation state unviable. Global telecommunications allow businesses to ignore national boundaries as they manipulate money and markets. Individual nations may amend interest rates and take other actions to protect their currency, but these usually are only as reaction to wider international events. Today, more and more national problems require international solutions.

Tribalism is a more human grouping than the nation, and as the union or alliances of states steadily grow, tribalism is also likely to grow. The perfect example of this tendency is to be seen in Africa, where the colonial nations established boundaries to suit themselves rather than the natural ethnicity of the area. Since the withdrawal of the European colonists, some twenty million people have died in Africa in what have been in essence tribal wars. The collapse of the Soviet Empire brought about a similar situation, again involving artificial boundaries, in the former Yugoslavia and the Caucasus. The next fifty years will be influenced by tribal disputes in Central and Southeastern Asia, Africa, and possibly Southern Europe.

Fundamentalism and Terrorism

The rise of fundamentalist religious groups and a variety of pseudoreligious fanatics has become a feature of recent history. Their growing use of terrorism to draw attention to their cause, justified or not, is a matter of grave concern to the governments of democratic countries. Now the real possibility of nuclear and chemical weapons of mass destruction coming into their hands has brought a new dimension to the issue: terrorists with unprecedented power in their hands. Many governments believe that international terrorism is more of a threat than the possibility of conventional war with other countries. It will remain an important issue for governments and businesses engaged in global trade for many years to come.

Europeans have been experiencing this phenomenon for some time and have grown in resilience and counterstrategies. Witness the British with the IRA, the French with Algerian Moslem groups such as the Armed Islamic Group (EIA) and the Islamic Solidarity Front (FIS), and the Germans with a more limited Turkish Moslem activity. For a long time, Americans saw terrorism as something that happened "over there," and they guarded against the arrival of terrorists from overseas. The slow realization that terrorist outrages at the World Trade Center in New York, the Oklahoma City disaster, and interruption of the Olympic Games in Atlanta were all perpetrated from within the United States came as a great shock.

Technology has given the advantage to the terrorist. The fact that readily available farm fertilizer was the main component of the Oklahoma bomb which killed so many is frightening enough.

But chemical weapons such as Semtex and Savin are available from Eastern Europe and the old Soviet Union. Semtex was used in massive explosions in London and elsewhere, and the nerve gas Savin was used to devastating effect in the Tokyo subway. These technologies provide relatively small groups with deadly weapons of mass destruction.

Now there is a more deadly possibility. Corruption, organized crime, and ill-paid soldiers are opening the nuclear arsenals of the old Soviet Union. Already there have been several cases of nuclear theft of bomb-grade goods that could be used to make an atomic bomb. Even the remote possibility of nuclear weapons in the hands of terrorists is a major challenge for the world. Of course, this level of technology is not of much help to small terrorist groups and probably needs the capital, technology, and desire of a fundamentalist dictator to be a practical threat. But how would the Gulf War alliance react if there were a repeat invasion of Kuwait by a Saddam Hussein with the stolen technology of intercontinental missiles and nuclear bombs? Clearly, finding an economic solution for Russia is needed to bring back security control.

Conclusion

The global economy continues to evolve and provide many opportunities for entrepreneurial companies both big and small. To succeed in this marketplace, three things are required:

1. A maintained knowledge base of how each area of operations is evolving and how opportunities are opening, for which products and services.
2. Competence in people, products, and the ability to compete at the highest levels and lowest price.
3. Alliances with other multinational companies and local operations, and with political and social leaders. This best ensures that the first two requirements are met and can be distributed in each market area.

A little like governments, the global corporation may have its own foreign office at home to maintain the focus. However, keep it very slim so as to avoid a new bureaucracy evolving.

Questions for the Reader

1. To what degree is senior management in your organization briefed on geopolitical events and trends?
2. How do you feel about the American Dream?
3. Do you believe that America is moving toward isolationism?
4. Have you or your company been involved with trading in the old Eastern bloc?
5. Did you know that the purchasing population (those likely to be in the market for consumer goods) of India is approximately 270 million, which is close to the total population of the United States?
6. Has your organization been felt an impact in its operations from international fundamentalism or terrorism?

Part Three

Simple Common Sense

These final chapters describe the simple common sense elements that go to make up the successful evolutionary organization: A framework of shared values with which the activities of the organization are maintained in balance with the aspirations of customers, employees, suppliers, owners and the community at large.

Chapter 9

Purpose

Great minds have purposes; others have wishes.
                    Washington Irving (1783–1859)

Though the Life Force supplies us with its own purpose, it has
no other brains to work with than those it has painfully and
imperfectly evolved in our heads.
                    George Bernard Shaw (1856–1950)

Lord Ronald . . . flung himself upon his horse and rode madly
off in all directions.
                    Nonsense Novels, Stephen Leacock (1869–1944)

Figure 9-1 illustrates the essential elements of the successful evolutionary organization. The main wheel represents the operations of the organization as a continuous circle or series of activities. These activities and the people involved in them are themselves evolving as the business grows. It could all be likened to a great orchestra preparing to produce that special sound that we all recognize as excellence. The leaders are orchestrating or conducting all these activities to ensure unity and to make certain that the players are not rushing madly off in all directions. But there is a complication. It is in the nature of business (and of life) that there is no precise score for the conductor to follow, because the score itself is also evolving. This is a recipe for bedlam.

As we have observed earlier, bedlam is too often the result of trying to come to terms with these disparate activities. We have

Figure 9-1. Framing the evolutionary circle.

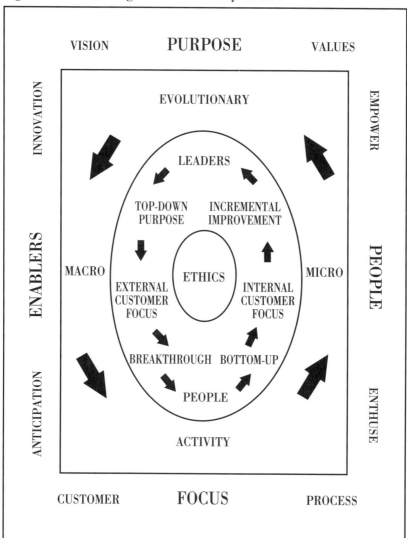

considered the Platonic answer, or the Taylor and scientific management approach to a carefully prescribed score based on the
principle of designing systems that minimize the effect of human
behavior. We have argued an alternative Aristotelian approach,
which recognizes the organic and evolving nature of *both* people
and the business: systems that complement and encourage the

positive aspects of human behavior in the environment. Rather than a prescribed score, the business orchestra requires a framework that can be shared by conductors and players alike, a framework of essential values, a clear focus on the essential, and an overall sense of purpose. Let's look a little more closely at the elements in Figure 9-1.

The Circle

In successful companies, the operational and planning activities are varied but not haphazard. As Figure 9-1 demonstrates, the activities are connected and *caused.* The majority are microactivities or processes as measured by their impact individually on the business. From time to time on the evolutionary circle, some of the activities have a macro effect on the success of the business. It is essential to realize that these are not activities that are better than the micro processes; indeed, in the evolutionary circle neither can exist without the other. Viewed holistically, the circle should be seen as a partnership between the organizational leaders and the people of the organization.

The leaders' role is to drive down through the organization the purpose of the organization. As a natural part of their role, leaders are strongly focused on the customer, the marketplace, and the future of the organization. As a result of that focus, from time to time they enunciate major breakthrough goals, substantially change company practices, or move the company dramatically into new product or market areas. Nevertheless, these "breakthrough" changes are still evolutionary rather than revolutionary as they are based on the wider perspective or framework for the organization.

The successful evolutionary organization that is designed for the long term does not only absorb the breakthrough but concentrates on maintaining, improving, and preparing these new activities for the next breakthrough. This key process tends to be driven by those involved in day-to-day implementation—in the shorthand of this book, the people. Their energies are released in continuous improvement of all processes in which they are involved. This pattern of incremental improvement enhances the credibility and performance of the organization and plays a crucial part in providing the platform for the next opportunity for a macro breakthrough. The continual revolving of this circle gradually evolves into a very powerful organization. But it needs a framework to keep it on course and to ensure that the wheel revolves to some purpose.

The Framework

The framework for the evolutionary circle illustrated in Figure 9-1 is in reality the subject of the ensuing chapters. The purpose of the organization, accompanying a clear vision or dream for its future together with a set of unifying values, is the subject of the latter part of this chapter. Chapter 10 examines how an evolutionary company maintains its focus on the customer and the processes that serve the customer. Involvement of people in the long-term success of the organization is examined in Chapter 12. All of these areas are essential to the success of any business, but there is a special arena that tends to differentiate the leading evolutionary companies. They use knowledge and what is happening around them to *enable* their operation to anticipate what is likely to support or to impede their evolution and then release the power of innovation to dominate their chosen market. We return to the hub of the wheel, ethics, which is growing as a key element for success in the global market. Chapter 13 develops the concept of ethics and stewardship as a growing facet needed for the future success of the evolutionary companies.

The four sides of the framework are held together by a glue, which can also be portrayed as the lubricant that allows smooth revolving of the evolutionary wheel—in other words, communication, which is the subject of Chapter 11.

Purpose and Values

Over the last few years, it has been fashionable for corporate executives to spend a weekend at a country retreat to develop a vision or purpose statement for their companies. A mishmash of consultants and would-be gurus have been eager to "facilitate" their deliberations. There is an implied promise behind all of this cerebral activity that publication of the vision and a set of matching values automatically sets the corporation along the right road to success. Nuts! For the majority of corporations (General Motors is a good example), this exercise has made little or no difference at all to their subsequent performance. It has been another exercise in mindless change.

But are we faced here with another paradox? There is ample evidence that all successful evolutionary companies have strong value systems and a clear sense of purpose. In reality, there is no paradox. The point is that evolutionary companies did not involve themselves in mechanistic exercises to create their visions and values. It would suit the theme of this book if it could be said that their values and vision simply evolved, but that's not true either. In the sense that as the organization grew there did become a need to share the vision with others, it could be seen as evolution. But in most cases the founder or group of founders had an innate sense of what *kind* of company they wanted to be. In other words, the foundation of so many great evolutionary companies that have stood the test of time is based more on values than on traditional business goals.

The early pronouncements of many founders of the great evolutionary companies support the preeminence of fundamental values as their original premises. Two powerful examples help make the point. Michael Marks, cofounder of the legendary Marks and Spencer, started with a cluster of penny bazaars in the markets of Northern England. Each market stall bore the sign "DON'T ASK THE PRICE—IT'S A PENNY." But he also said, "They expect value for their hard-earned penny." Sam Walton, the founder of Wal-Mart, stated, "I had no vision of the scope of what I would start. . . . But I had confidence that as long as we did our work well and were good to our customers there would be no limit to us."

None of these organizations opened with great visionary statements such as "My dream is to build Europe's greatest retailer." Very few major, lasting corporations started with some great technological breakthrough or with the purpose of creating some colossus of business. They started with a set of cherished notions and beliefs that would guide every move that the company made in the future—in other words, a value system.

The concept of a set of guiding values as being at the heart of, and essential to, the long-term successful organization now appears proven and accepted by the leading proponents of management thought. It is more difficult to accept as proven when these same advisers proclaim as a corollary that these corporations have a vision, in the sense of a super goal, that drives them forward. Some of the lasting corporations certainly do have such visions. But equally, many certainly do not express their sense of purpose through a vision or purpose statement. For example, Arthur Andersen, 3M, Marks and Spencer, Honeywell, and J. Sainsbury do not communicate with their employees or the rest of the world in that manner. Interestingly, two of them started in industries that have little to do with those in which they rose to leadership. Yet all of these corporations had a clear *sense* of purpose that has guided them.

The difference between the two approaches could be said to come from the choice between two missing words in the following definition of purpose:

A dramatic and complete picture of _____ the company wants to be

If your choice is "where," then establish a vision statement that drives the company forward to that destination. If your choice is "what," then concentrate on focusing on the set of values that make up the what. With the latter choice, the effort to bring together these beliefs into one dramatic statement could obscure some of the values. But none of the above precludes an organization's having strategies, goals, and best practices.

Strategies, Goals, and Practices

Successful companies do have clear strategies or definition of methods by which they meet their business goals. In some cases, these goals may appear visionary in the sense that they are great leaps forward accompanied by substantial risk. They also promote best practices as a way of keeping their values in focus. But the most important characteristic of an evolutionary company is that all these strategies, goals, and practices are subject to change, whereas their values do not change. In reality, the fundamental values are used as a reference point to test the validity of goals and strategies. They use their inculcated values as a compass in managing change and anticipating *their* future. We return to this theme in Chapter 13, on stewardship.

A word of warning for those attracted to the case-history method of learning about management. Many organizations are run for the greater glory of the CEO or leader. In those and other situations where the public relations spin doctors hold sway, hindsight can be manipulated; to quote Thomas Carlyle, "History is a distillation of rumor." Clearly expressed strategies and goals are often discovered afterwards to explain what has happened. They are used to convince today's observers that the skipper has always had a clear vision and a firm hand on the tiller.

Breakthrough Goals

Since the advent of Hammer and business process reengineering, establishing breakthrough goals has been all the fashion. The whole movement can be summed up in two admonitions: "Think outside the box" and "Think the unthinkable." Of course, the phrases are intended to give designers permission to question authority and the limits of existing systems and to identify false assumptions; in that sense, they are harmless. Evolutionary firms by their nature usually empower employees to act that way. However, it is clear that much breakthrough activity, as we discussed earlier, has had disastrous effects on corporations and their people. Some of those disasters come from the mindless changes that emanate from those phrases.

It is precisely because they think *inside* the box that evolutionary companies are successful. They take great care to create a box or value system that maintains focus and provides the horizons for thought. Such companies do not want their horses riding wildly off in all directions. And *to think the unthinkable* is a phrase that can only seriously come from those who are not thinking and are eager for another bout of revolutionary change. Because they continuously anticipate change and "think the thinkable," evolutionary companies are always close to reality and command the loyalty and respect of their customers and employees. The unthinkable is almost always also the "undo-able." Once again, it is the difference in philosophy between Plato and Aristotle.

The Right Way to Success

The common denominator for our evolutionary companies is a culture based on a set of accepted values. If that, then, is the right way to success, what is the right set of values? For starters, there is no *right way* to succeed. If there is one common thing about the companies we have discussed, it is that they do not have a common set of values or even a common way of doing things. They have each evolved from a different set of circumstances and grown in differing industries or environments. They have become *themselves*; they are not based upon a role model. For the same reason, they should not be copied as role models in the case-history sense. The lesson they teach us is that it is essential to have the confidence to be oneself. The pursuit of business is not unlike the pursuit of life, of which it is a part.

It is not just that the values of these corporations are different but that in some cases they are diametrically different. In the slow move away from the command-and-control approach to management, there has been a tendency to believe that there is a need to establish *soft* values. There is a need for values that understand the concept of care, but it would be difficult to accept that meritocracy, which is one of Arthur Andersen's values, is in any way a soft value. The firm expresses that value in these terms: "We provide our people with challenging opportunities for career advancement based on their effectiveness in serving the client." In that context, new entrants quickly recognize that the word *effectiveness* is very important and is far from soft.

For the organization that has a desire to emulate evolutionary companies, the first step should be to take time and care to assess their current culture. The assessment should concentrate on the *characteristics* of decision making and employee reactions. These should help to determine the *perceptions* of everyone involved in what they think are the dominant values. It is foolhardy to attempt to change or modify corporate values without a very clear understanding of the innate values that are currently driving the organization. Only then can there be any estimation of the delta between actuality and desire. This book is not arguing against change; clearly, many corporations do need to change. The argument is that change needs very careful and applied thought; unfortunately, too many well-intentioned executives have been seduced into mindless change. The assessment also indicates not only what may need changing but perhaps more importantly which existing shared values need greater emphasis or support.

Action Counts

The power of words can bring about change, but more usually action counts in establishing the fruits of change. How management behaves in a change situation counts for far more than any mission statements that may be produced. It is also worth noting that these actions do not, any more than values, need to be nice or kind actions. Deep down, employees and even customers know what is wrong with a company however much they may like some of its characteristics. "I have nothing to offer but blood, toil, tears, and sweat," said Winston Churchill as his opening statement as prime minister in May 1940. Hardly a beautiful vision of the new dream to come. This was an occasion when words did have the power of action. Instantly, the British people (and many others around the world) knew that something different was happening; the drift and indecision were over.

So what actions should the CEO take to make it very clear that something different is happening? There are no simple answers, but based on earlier chapters about what is wrong with mindless management I offer the following:

⊙ *Sell the chateau.* Clear the purposeful fog and bring decision making closer to real action. This could be demonstrated to powerful effect by closing the existing corporate headquarters and establishing a new pattern of operational management.

⊙ *Disperse the supporting processes.* Do not denigrate the importance of having the best support areas, such as HR, PR, IT, and general administration. However, it does have to be made clear that the essential operations of the company are what the business is about. Subject to actions below, these processes may retain their professional independence but should report to the CEO *through* operational executives.

⊙ *Retain a strong financial core.* Ensure that the CEO and key operational executives have strong financial advice and collaboration with financial sources. However, also ensure that financial administration such as budgeting, billing, payments, expenses, etc., are dispersed to relevant operational areas.

⊙ *Establish an independent audit function.* This function should be conceived as being much wider than a financial audit function. Depending upon the business, there are many processes and strategies that could benefit from an independent audit reporting to the CEO. This function could also provide an ideal vehicle for development of potential leaders in understanding the operations and values of the corporation.

⊙ *Establish a knowledge and or culture center.* This center could be seen as part of the CEO's office, but it must be accessible to and indeed be proactively involved with all the functions of the corporation. Its primary objectives are to ensure universal understanding of the values of the company and to provide the knowledge briefing on all the issues that could affect the future of the business. It is a living library for the corporation.

⊙ *Establish an operational review of all contracts and legal procedures.* The purpose of this review is to ensure that all contracts are simple and represent a *fair deal for all parties.* Eliminate all clauses that are designed to limit your liability. Trust the law, not the lawyers. The millions saved in legal fees far outweigh the risks; and remember at the same time that you are establishing trust and a bond with your customers and suppliers. Incidentally, you are doing your bit to reduce the number of lawyers!

⊙ *Establish an operational review of all policies and procedures.* In particular, review personnel policies and forms of remuneration. Eliminate or modify all that inhibit risk, constrain empowerment, or are likely to stultify innovation. Employees have a right to know what is expected of them, and of course many procedures are defined by external regulation, but personnel policies should be driven by trust and designed to encourage self-esteem and confidence.

Conclusion

It is self-evident that a sense of purpose derived from a shared and inculcated set of values is the common factor in all evolutionary companies. It is also clear that only those companies that are determined to find their *own* value system can hope to emulate evolutionary companies. Having a sense of purpose and agreed principles upon which to operate is only common sense.

Questions for the Reader

1. What would you consider are the top four values of your company?
2. Can you describe the purpose of your company without having to refer to any official document?
3. What action would prove to you that your company wants to be evolutionary?
4. What do you perceive as the best characteristics of your company in relation to others?
5. Why do you work for your present company?

Chapter 10

Focus

Depend upon it, Sir, when a man knows that he is to be hanged in a fortnight, it concentrates his mind wonderfully.

Samuel Johnson (1709–1784)

Do not do unto others as you would they should do unto you. Their tastes may not be the same.

George Bernard Shaw (1856–1950)

One sees great things from the valley; only small things from the peak.

G. K. Chesterton (1874–1936)

In the preceding chapter, we noted that few great evolutionary companies had started with a great vision of where they were going. Of course, many companies are started with a new idea or invention, a new product or a new approach to service. A few succeed, but most fail for one reason or another to reach the big time. They are often eaten up by marauding tigers on the lower foothills of their visionary mountain. A clear purpose or vision and values alone are not enough for success.

There are three other elements that go together to make for success. These are luck, competence, and focus. It is amazing how many believe that luck is an essential element, particularly among those who have failed. But it is also amazing how unfair life and business really are, because most of the luck seems to go to those with purpose, competence, and an unremitting focus. Personal experience supports the thesis. There is an element in my personality that is always looking for something new (perhaps deep down I am a revolutionary attempting to break free from reasonable evolution). I have pioneered in a number of areas of both business and politics. I have failed more often than I have succeeded, but in truth I would admit that the failures were all due to incompetence in some sector or a failure to maintain focus on the key issues at the right time.

Between competence and focus, the latter is the more important. An unrelenting focus on customers and the key process in delighting customers quickly identifies incompetence. The truly focused leader compensates for personal incompetence in specific areas through advisors and the colleagues he or she selects. Within the total organization, incompetence should be countered by recruitment and the level of education and training provided. As we shall see, focus also highlights the issues of the corporation's core competencies.

Charismatic Leaders

Charismatic leaders are usually highly focused and can turn their whole personality to a vision. They are also very competent individuals in recognizable areas. Yet the great evolutionary corporations rarely select such people as their CEOs. Other substantial companies have turned occasionally, often under pressure from Wall Street, to charismatic personalities as a savior in difficult times. The reason probably lies in aiming to maintain the continuous balance between purpose, competence, and focus. Charismatic leaders, almost without exception, have an ego problem. They have been proved so right in the past that they automatically see disagreement as some kind of obscurantist opposition. As a result, they tend to surround themselves with "one of us" types of people who lack the same qualities of purpose, competency, and focus. The charismatic leader can enthuse a company or even a nation by the sheer force of personality *for a period*, but the evolutionary company is playing for the long-term. Perhaps Jack Welch is an exception to the rule in that as the CEO of General Electric he is one of the most charismatic leaders in the United States. However, Welch is a product of GE and presumably inculcated with the power of GE's value systems.

The Essentials

A recurring theme of this book is that the message our education systems and business schools should impart is the relative simplicity of business. There is a tendency to concentrate on technical aspects of financial management and obscure the essentials in detail. The simple essentials are (1) customer focus (little else matters; without customers there is no business) and (2) process focus (concentrate on those processes that are involved with the customer). These essentials are the counterpoint to the mindless changes highlighted in the first part of this book. All those changes were the result of introspective thinking that had lost sight of the commonsense elements of success.

Business survival, let alone success, depends on strategies, products, and services that are directed at delighting customers. This statement is a truism that most executives readily accept. Unfortunately, not enough realize that to achieve that level of customer focus, they need to *talk* to customers. They believe that they know the business and therefore know what the customer wants. But customer perceptions of their own needs are constantly changing.

Figure 10-1 indicates the degree to which customer perceptions have changed since the onslaught of global competition. In the 1960s, the seller's market meant that customers were satisfied if the product just worked most of the time. The Japanese

Figure 10-1. Customer quality perceptions.

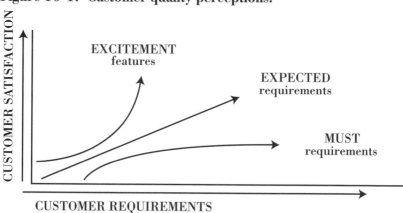

changed that customer perception, and the expected requirements began to include the way customers were invoiced, the way queries were handled, and other elements of service surrounding the product.

Increasing competition and the resulting rise in customer expectations has now reached a new level on the satisfaction index; we now discuss a customer focus that delights the customer or, as we see in Figure 10-1, provides features that excite the customer. This requires that the corporation so organize and focus its customer-oriented processes that everybody learns to walk in the customer's shoes.

An experience with Virgin Airways provides a good example of what is meant by customer focus. As a customer of Virgin's Upper Class service, I was at home waiting for the limousine that Virgin provides to and from the airport when I received a telephone call from Virgin: "Mr. Macdonald, we are sorry to tell you that your flight to Boston will be delayed by up to two hours. Would you prefer to spend that time at home or be picked up immediately?" None-too-pleased, I opted for the time at home, and the Virgin representative continued: "We have noted from your ticketing that you were using Boston as a transit stop on the way to Chicago. We have checked with our Boston people, and we are certain that we can make that connection. We will handle your baggage separately, you will be first off the plane, and our representative will meet you and take you through VIP immigration to your connecting flight." I had by then moved my perception from annoyance at inconvenience to being impressed with Virgin's attempts to put things right. Then followed the real evidence of customer focus. Their representatives had stepped into the customer's shoes and envisaged the issues surrounding the delay. "Sir, with your planned stopover, had you intended meeting or phoning colleagues in Boston? If so, could we (Virgin) phone them and explain that it is our fault that this will not be possible?" A dissatisfied customer has now become a delighted customer. There were no bribes or sweeteners to keep the customer happy but instead a series of communications both within the organization and to the customer to ensure the excitement feature. That is customer focus. It comes from that old-fashioned virtue of *knowing* the customer and attending to his or her *personal* needs. Customer focus comes from that customer knowledge.

Knowing the Customer

Communicating with customers has to be considered, planned, and organized activity. Too often, management is satisfied only with the quick-fix solution of customer-care training for receptionists and others who talk directly with customers so that they are courteous and caring. This does not suffice in today's competitive marketplace. Here, we concentrate on the four key elements of customer focus, namely:

1. *Marketing*: Who are our customers, and what are their needs and desires?
2. *Promotion*: Let the customers know that we have solutions to their needs.
3. *Selling*: Agree, and contract, to meet the personal needs of individual customers.
4. *Service*: Provide the after-sales service and care that creates lifetime customers.

Conventional wisdom tends to combine the first three elements as disparate parts of marketing. That is, however, a major fallacy in business.

Marketing

Marketing is responsible for researching and defining the products and services that delight customers. Marketing has little or nothing to do with promoting or selling products and services. Thus, research and development is part of the marketing function, but selling is not.

The communication methods used by the marketing department to carry out its primary functions in customer focus can be summarized as follows:

- Customer and market surveys
- Customer focus groups
- Relations with special customers
- Competitive intelligence

Customer and Market Surveys

Consumer surveys and questionnaires are the most prevalent method of seeking customers and prospect views because they:

- Are cheap
- Are relatively easy to organize
- Are easy to process
- Provide demographic data

However, this form of communication is only partly effective. Customer surveys rarely provide the level of input required. Unless the customer experience has been very bad, the overall input is generally good enough to create a feeling of comfort. But a new competitor could dramatically change the survey evaluation. Surveys suffer from generalization, whereas marketing strategy is dependent on specifics.

A survey gathers quasi-factual information and demographic date for analysis. It also allows limited feedback from the customer and may help to identify future members of focus groups. However, the approach suffers from lack of interaction with the recipients and takes little account of their perceptions. Customer perceptions about the use of data linked to their identity can lead them to fantasize or even lie about their own status and desires.

Some of these weaknesses in surveys can be overcome by careful formulation and juxtaposition of questions, but usually at the cost of sacrificing brevity. At best, this method of communicating with customers should be used sparely, and only to indicate trends or to identify areas for more in-depth research. As we see later, technology now provides more powerful tools for collecting useful data.

Customer Focus Groups

The focus group is one of the most powerful communication tools available to marketing. It can provide both subjective and objective information. By their very nature, focus groups *involve* the customer both in research and, to some extent, in decisions. Competently managed, they can provide an intuitive perspective that can be as relevant as the analytical data. Successful management of customer focus groups is dependent on three areas:

1. *The composition of the group*: The first determinant for selection of the group members is the intended *focus* of the marketeer. This ranges from overall evaluation of perceived service to acceptability of an intended new product. The set-up therefore varies between a group representing the overall customer base to a more tightly selected group representing a specific market sector. Experience has shown that seven to nine members constitute the most effective focus groups. Focus groups are not to be confused with market opinion groups. The latter are designed for relatively large audiences that provide more interaction than do written questionnaires.

2. *The organization of the venue*: We want to encourage discussion and elicit opinions rather than deliver information. This requires a relaxed and nonconfrontational environment. The advice is to avoid formal boardroom-style layouts and "threatening" devices such as tape recorders. On the positive side, provide constant informal access to light refreshments.

3. *The selection of the facilitator*: Facilitating *meaningful* discussion is a highly skilled competence that requires training and experience. If that expertise does not exist in the organization, seek outside help.

Relations with Special Customers

All businesses have key account customers who provide a combination of revenue and market credibility and as a result are accorded special attention. There is nothing wrong with this, but it can be a source of conflict between selling and marketing. The salesforce aims to keep the customer focused on the immediate sales situation. It wants to keep close to the customer and control all communication. Outsiders, such as marketing, are seen as a complication to be avoided. Marketing sees the same customers as providing a "partnership of interest" in defining the future and thus also wants to get close. Both functions have laudable objectives, but they can appear to be in conflict. Here, the chief executive has a crucial role to play in resolving any perceived conflict and in ensuring successful communication with special customers.

Competitive Intelligence

Competitive intelligence is not to be confused with industrial espionage. Knowing the other side of the hill has always been essential for the world's leading companies. Of the two elements of gaining and analyzing intelligence, the first is clearly a communications exercise. A whole book could be devoted to this subject, but from my experience, a useful start would be to combine an ambitious new M.B.A. graduate and a qualified librarian within the marketing department. The former has knowledge of business and an eager desire to "find out," and the latter has the professional training required to manage information.

Promotion

The convergence of technologies is increasing the scope of customer communication, even though some of the devices involved are not perceived as being related to communication. We noted one such technique in Chapter 7 which Texaco used to develop detailed data on the behavior of millions of customers. This use of communication is to the advantage of both parties. Figure 10-1 indicated the growing need for "excitement features." There is a dangerous temptation for promotional operations to meet this need by inventing excitement. In fairness, they can also be led into this practice by claims of marketing about a new product, as for example with the fiasco over Unilever's claims about the new power of their washing powder Persil or Omo (as it is known in some countries). There are regulatory bodies to control some of these claims, but most are relatively toothless.

A principle of the marketplace (the arena for communicating with customers) is: All that customers want is what they have been promised. Promises are made to customers in promoting and selling products and services, and management should be alert to *dubious* promises made in advertising, packaging, and other promotional activities. Almost without exception, false promises made in the excitement of the moment come back to haunt the organization. They also cost a lot of money: The quick buck now is usually paid for later.

In communicating with customers, promotional or marketing flair should not be confused with false promises. Imagination and flair are essential and positive elements in successful communication. The "white paint war" of a few years ago provides a perfect example of such flair. For a long period, the paint market was dominated by the perceived need to be "whitest." Reflective agents were added to paint, and advertising copywriters came up with "whiter than white." These were impossible parameters to communicate to customers, and so inevitably the whole market became involved in a costly price war. Then, with a touch of pigment and an intuitive feel for customer perceptions, a marketing manager in the British giant Imperial Chemical Industries (ICI) created "not quite white"—which could be sold at a higher price. She transformed ICI's profit margins and market share, and all ICI's competitors then played follow the leader.

But as all these examples indicate, a high focus on customers must be supported by an equal focus on the company people and processes that are designed to deliver excitement to the customer.

Customer vs. Internal Focus

The whole discussion about customer focus can be illustrated by two simple diagrams. In Figure 10-2 we see the typical organization. All the employees are fixed on satisfying their management rather than the customers; nobody is listening to or even looking at the customers.

In this environment, top management is sitting in the chateau focused on profit and cost containment. Middle management is concentrating on productivity and developing company control policies, procedures, and practices. The frontline people, who have direct contact with the customers, are working in

Figure 10-2. Internal focus.

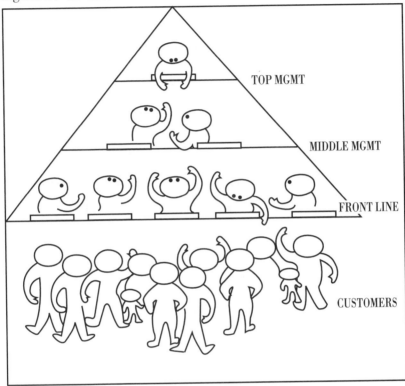

fear of appraisals, reorganization, and having to satisfy supervisors rather than customers. In this company-oriented world, all the old jokes are appropriate:

> ***Customer:*** I need film for this camera.
> ***Salesperson:*** I'm sorry sir, we used to sell that film, but we were always running out, so we don't stock it anymore.

In the customer-focused organization (Figure 10-3), the pyramid is reversed and the whole company is turned toward the customer. Throughout the corporation, reward and recognition is determined more by how workers delight customers than by how they satisfy supervisors. Management is concentrating on developing customer-friendly products and procedures. Top management is focused on creating the organizational structure

Figure 10-3. Customer focus.

and the financial resources to support the organization's customer focus.

Process Focus

In Chapter 2, we discussed the key processes of business and realized that a lot of management time and focus is dispersed across a series of issues that are not essential to the success of business. Process focus is the positive reaction to those problems. In essence, process focus has two facets: (1) ensuring that the strategies, policies, procedures, and practices of the company are oriented to supporting the people and processes that directly delight customers, and (2) ensuring that focus is on the day-to-day measures of process capability and improvement rather than on one-off, after-the-event financial measures.

To a large extent, process focus comes as a result of the purpose and values of the organization as implemented through the education and training of all the people involved. We touch on these areas in the next chapter. But the day-to-day focus of the organization comes from people's perception of what is important to senior management. Some of that perception is formed from specific statements of management, and policy initiatives. However, the most powerful influence on perceptions comes from the questions that management asks and its reactions to the answers.

A Business Model for Focus

Business can be represented as a simple division between the enablers and the results. The key processes of the organization drive results, and so the key to business is to pursue excellence in all the enablers.

The European Foundation for Quality Management (EFQM) is a voluntary association of major industries across Europe to promote the concepts of quality throughout European companies, large and small. The foundation has developed a model (see Figure 10-4) that graphically represents the concept and provides a basis for companies to assess their own performance against international criteria.

The EFQM business model is widely used in the United Kingdom and the countries of the European Union in the drive toward excellence and competitiveness in the global market. There is growing evidence to show that organizations that score well in assessments against the EFQM model deliver outstanding business results. It therefore follows that using the model's criteria as an initial focus point leads to improved business performance.

The basic principles of the model illustrated in Figure 10-4 are straightforward. Leadership (1) drives policy and strategy (2).

Figure 10-4. European Foundation for Quality Management (EFQM) business model.

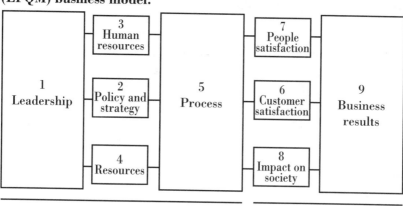

Enablers   Results

In that process, it also develops or reinforces the purpose and values of the organization. The leaders of the organization then concentrate on organizing the resources (4) at their command, including the people (3), through the operational processes (5) of the company. These processes serve both to increase customer satisfaction (6) and people satisfaction (7). Increasingly business is involved in the positive impact it can have on society (8). This last process indicates that the EFQM model is well designed for the perspectives of tomorrow. Maintaining a balanced focus on all these areas ultimately produces business results (9). All in all, this is a pretty good analysis of the evolutionary company we have been discussing.

Benchmarking

The EFQM model has been described as a benchmark for business. The concept of benchmarking is changing the perspective of executives and managers around the world. It is showing them how good, bad, or mediocre their company is in aspects of their own business as compared with world-class companies.

The growth of benchmarking has been so rapid, and the experience of its use so diverse, that there is confusion as to what the term covers. Some see it merely as an extension of competitive analysis. In truth, however, benchmarking can provide realistic measures and goals for *every* process in the company; in addition, benchmarking spotlights the practices behind company performance.

Although the concept of benchmarking is quite simple, the full implications and applications of the technique are rarely understood. An example of what is *really* meant by benchmarking is that of a coal-mining company that performed a study using Disney World in Florida as their benchmarking partner. It is difficult to think of two companies with more divergent interest (despite the seven mining dwarfs in *Snow White*). What the coal company was studying was the way in which Disney maintained the pneumatics within their animated robot characters. Clearly, Disney cannot allow their attractions to lose their lifelike appeal for even a few minutes, so they have developed world-class maintenance routines for their air-pneumatics systems. The mining company studied these routines and was able to *adapt* elements back into their own processes. The resulting decrease in downtime resulted in a major improvement in productivity.

In Western management, the benchmarking pioneer is recognized as Robert C. Camp, as a result of his book on the subject published in 1989; however, as we noted in Chapter 4, benchmarking was being used in Japan long before. There it was developed in several forms and had more to do with their success than with any foreign gurus such as Deming. Benchmarking is the natural tool of evolutionary companies. It keeps them focused on customers and processes and helps them adapt to every new use of technology or its convergence.

Innovation

Successful innovation is increasingly seen as the key to sustained commercial success and competitive advantage. Innovation is not the same as invention; some of the greatest innovations of recent times have been the result of taking existing and proven technologies and combining them in ways that transformed the market. The Sony Walkman is a perfect example of this convergence. The development of the Post-It note at another evolutionary company, 3M, was an innovative response to an adhesive developed by research and development chemists that wasn't sticky enough for its intended purpose.

Innovation is also not just the result of a lucky hunch; it can be encouraged and managed to achieve success. Clearly, innovation does not thrive in a bureaucratic organization or one where barriers to change, such as fear, exist. Generally, it thrives in companies that exhibit the confidence of strong values, trust, and encouragement to take risks and make individual decisions. Another element is fostering of eyes that see and ears that hear, as well as continuous counting of the greens in technology and best practices. Innovative companies establish partnerships of interest with their customers and suppliers; these relationships help to spur innovative thought. As we have noted before, evolutionary companies are continuously asking questions, which in itself leads to innovation.

Conclusion

In all successful evolutionary companies, there is a focus that permeates the whole organization. Management makes it clear that they value the principles that have been established. By the measurement criteria they establish and the continual thrust of their questions and interest, they make it very clear that the customer is the primary concern of the corporation.

Questions for the Reader

1. What is the key customer-oriented policy in your organization?
2. What is the most anticustomer procedure that you have experienced?
3. In your day-to-day life, can you name the company that has most delighted you?
4. How does or did that company differ from others?
5. What would you most like to see introduced into your company?
6. Is benchmarking used in your organization?
7. Are you encouraged to innovate and take the risk of doing something unusual?

Chapter 11

Communication

One can live in the shadow of an idea without grasping it.
>   Elizabeth Bowen (1899–1973)

Talking and eloquence are not the same: to speak, and to speak well, are two things.
>   Ben Johnson (1573–1637)

Presidents, executives, and coworkers: Lend me your ears.
>   *Hemispheres*, Diana Corley Schnapp

If value systems are the heart of successful organizations, then communication is the blood that brings life to every limb of the operation. Communication with customers, employees, suppliers, shareholders, and the community at large is what business is all about. Communication is a process that applies equally to manufacturing, service, and public-sector organizations. In today's global market, successful communication cannot ignore but must instead transcend the barriers of language and culture.

Technology has created a rapidly increasing ability for an ever larger number of people to communicate relatively freely with one another. Yet that very freedom to communicate, allied with constant increase in the pace and amount of communication, has exposed a series of barriers to successful communication. What once appeared to be a simple process has now become a complex and confusing issue for those involved in work.

In the business environment, communication plays a vital

role in ensuring that things get done. To avoid costly misunderstandings and time delays, communication is thus formal in nature and must be carefully planned and organized to be successful. Unfortunately, this is far from common practice in modern organizations. A consultant was advising a large corporation involved in the packaging industry. He was impressed with the participatory management style evident in the corporate offices. On a visit to an operational location, he asked the plant manager what he thought of the open and frank communication style in the corporation. The reply was illuminating: "In this company, we communicate openly and frankly about everything—except about making boxes." Making boxes was, of course, their business. That is the issue; communication should be about making boxes (or whatever our business actually is) and indeed about making the very best boxes that will delight the market.

Barriers to Communication

Current management practices inhibit clear, concise, and direct communication of the information needed to get things done successfully. Some of them create barriers to communication between levels of management as well as between departmental peers at each level. Other barriers are created by individual perceptions of the parties to communication, and by fostered cultures of organizations. The major barriers to communication were touched upon in the early chapters and can be summarized as:

- Specialization and departmental fortresses
- Division between the thinkers and the doers
- Tradition, culture, and status
- Hidden dynamics—emotions at work
- National myopias and perceptions
- Lack of a common language

The first two of these barriers were discussed in Chapter 2, but the others are worth examining as the basis for developing a worthwhile communications strategy.

Tradition, Culture, and Status

All too often, and despite their best attempts at successful communication strategy, most executives fail to see the hidden barriers to communication that are based on individual perceptions of tradition, culture, and status.

Individuals formulate or interpret a message according to their own perception of "what goes on around here" or "what they really meant." New executives may not recognize that a long tradition of authoritarian communications from on high has established cynical mistrust of all management messages. Customers of a public utility may not trust the statements of the perceived "fat cat." These perceptions can actually create gaps in communication because the intended recipients turn off and do not listen to the message. In our prevailing organizational culture, executives, managers, and employees all exhibit behavior patterns that create these gaps:

Executives

- Often communicate decisions with little or no knowledge of the implication of their decisions for the company or the people who have to implement decisions
- Fail to communicate effectively; are bad at explaining decisions
- Send *different* messages to shareholders than to staff
- Work as individuals, not as teams, and call for teamwork throughout the organization but exclude themselves
- Rarely "walk the talk"; exhort the workforce to adhere to values that they themselves blatantly ignore
- Fail to establish measurable criteria for anything other than short-term financial or people management; do not know what is going on
- Fail to lead; too often remote from their organizations

Managers

- Feel stressed or overstretched in implementing executive decisions
- Lack enthusiasm for change; have been let down before
- Fail to collaborate or practice teamwork with their peers

- Create a "purposeful fog" that inhibits communication
- Ape executives in actions; lack measurement and fail to lead

Employees

- Are left in the dark, victims of the mushroom management joke
- Feel at the bottom of the pit, with no one else left to hit
- Feel skeptical and mistrusting
- Feel unheard and unappreciated
- Are consequently unable to release their potential; tend to construct defense mechanisms

These behavior patterns are based on perceptions or beliefs that are themselves assumptions about what is true. The trouble with organizational behavior is that such perceptions quickly become facts, because people tend to communicate and act within the framework of their perceptions.

Hidden Dynamics: Emotions at Work

The traditional "rational" world of business believes that our emotions are better kept private. Faith Ralston, author of *Hidden Dynamics,* argues that this is a dangerous misconception, and that, like it or not, human feelings affect every job and organization. Too often at work, we try to stifle our feelings; yet even in a business environment, our emotional needs can be harnessed for positive communication and positive results. To understand and deal with the dynamic nature of emotions in the workplace, she argues that the following eight principles are important to keep in mind:

1. Emotional needs always express themselves one way or another.
2. Anger is an expression of need.
3. Our feelings and needs are not wrong or bad.
4. Emotions are the gateway to vitality and feeling alive.
5. We can address our emotions and still save face.

6. Immediate reactions to problems often disguise deeper feelings.
7. We must clarify individual needs before problem solving with others.
8. We need to communicate both positive and negative feelings.

National Myopias and Perceptions

National cultures or particular uses of language can create major blind spots or false perceptions that hinder clear, concise, and direct communication by large corporations. In most cases, the perpetrators of these communication blunders remain in blissful ignorance of the damage they are causing. They are imprisoned in a national myopia. The vast need for increased global communication in business highlights this as an area of growing concern in successful communication. We have all laughed from time to time at bizarre stories of international miscommunication. These mishaps are usually obvious, but there are a host of others that go unrecognized by the senders and so continue to sow discord and misconception.

Lack of a Common Language

An area of language difficulty in business communication that is not so readily recognized is the different "languages" used by executives, management, and workers. Executives are reputed to be concerned about only three issues: 1) making money, 2) not losing money, and 3) money! Although this is perhaps not totally fair, it does serve to illustrate a serious issue in internal business communication. Workers on their part do *not* talk in the language of money but instead in the language of things and getting things done. They may be interested in their paychecks, but they are not much concerned with revenue and profit ratios. Yet too often executives talk to workers in the language of business finance and assume that the latter know what is happening. Middle managers are caught in between as they attempt to talk both languages and often just end up confusing everybody.

To achieve purposeful communication within organizations, we need to use a common language to overcome barriers of status or function. The most successful organizations use the language of processes and measurement to communicate effectively about "making boxes" or getting things done.

Media and Message

In many instances in modern technology, it is difficult to escape the conclusion that the medium has become more important than the message. Too often, senders are more concerned with demonstrating their prowess with the latest technology than they are to ensure that the recipient has received and understood the intended message. Having said that, I add that an essential element of successful communication is selecting and using the media best suited to both the message and the recipients. Some typical examples of misuse or bad selection of media at conferences and other large-scale communication (which most of us have experienced) that create interference with the message are:

- Use of overhead transparencies coupled with standard-sized screens at large conferences; no one but the speaker can see a thing, and the message is lost.
- Overcrowded transparencies, which produce the same result.
- Back projection of 35mm slides controlled by separate operator using a scripted speech. In concentrating on not missing the key words, the speaker loses all spontaneity and rapport with the audience.
- TV and other advertisements that appear to be competing for in-group prizes rather than selling the product to the target buyers; the message here is drowned in clever visual tricks and layouts.
- E-mail messages or memos that are sent indiscriminately to "complete" lists without checking their relevance to each individual recipient. These create so much "noise in the channel" that important messages are obscured.
- Overreliance on the ability of technology to handle error correction with ease, which is conducive to lazy formula-

tion of messages and to the expectation that someone else will spot errors and make relevant corrections. In some organizations, the major impact of computers has been just to move communication errors around both more quickly and to a wider audience. "Right the first time" should be a principle of all communication.

Communications Methodology

Successful business communication depends on clear methodology based on three principles:

1. Understanding the category, characteristics, and environment of the intended recipient of our message
2. Selecting the ideal media both to fit the message content and to meet the recipient's needs
3. Formulating the message and the form of presentation so as to maximize the advantages of the medium selected

This methodology presupposes that the message is worthwhile and that the recipient is predisposed to receive the message. The principles are not intended to be a form of bureaucratic procedure to be followed for every message we wish to communicate in day-to-day business operations. Rather, they should be seen as elements in a thinking process that should become automatic.

Understanding the Recipient

Lack of comprehension of the first principle above probably accounts for the majority of mistakes in business communication. The higher we rise in the organizational hierarchy, the more likely we are to send messages that are doomed to be misunderstood. Senior managers may have a message that they want to convey to all those involved in an issue. In the haste to communicate in a timely fashion, the disparate characteristics of the recipients and the environments in which they work are ignored. More typically, the message is adulterated and compromised for a

wider audience. Perception differs with each category of recipient. The issue becomes clearer when we appreciate the differing
characteristics and working environments of all the following,
who are normal recipients of some form of business communication:

owners	shareholders
boards of directors	senior managers
managers and supervisors	specialists and technologists
corporate staff	field staff
sales force	sales support staff
administrative workers	manufacturing workers
key material suppliers	in-house service suppliers
other suppliers	consultants
key account customers	prospects
other customers	trade associations
trade press	other press and media
regulatory bodies	local government
central government	community

Additionally, in this politically correct world we have to take
into account differences of gender, nationality, race, and even
sexual orientation. As if that were not enough, we also have to
consider the overall communication environment before we select our medium. Some of the possibilities are:

one-to-one	versus	selected groups
en masse	versus	face-to-face
direct	versus	indirect
verbal	versus	visual image
one-shot	versus	repetitive
natural environment	versus	designed environment

In the language of communication, the last pair here is often
referred to as "your place or mine."

Choice of Media

The modern business communicator has access to a wide choice
of media for distributing a message. In theory, this should assist

in matching the right medium both to the message and to the recipient. In practice, however, it is not as simple as that. Many of the media listed below need skilled interpreters or are not under the control of the principal communicator:

national press and TV	local press and TV
in-house magazines	trade press
in-house conferences or seminars	external conferences
team briefings	staff or union meetings
memoranda	e-mail and the Internet
telephone	faxes
letters	"business lunches"*
committees	meetings

A medium that seems opportune is too often selected without due consideration of message and recipients. The above list of media is by no means exhaustive, but if allied to the list of conceivable recipients it does add to the seeming complexity of making mix-and-match decisions.

Management Attitudes

Management—and in particular British management—is very suspicious about communication. Most managers recognize in principle the need for communication with staff, suppliers, and customers. However, in practice, they lack confidence and are concerned about need to know, leaks to competition or the press, and the possibility that premature announcements will leave them looking foolish. As a result, many corporate communication programs become one-way vehicles for propaganda.

Management hates to convey negative information—such as possible layoffs resulting from recent mergers—since it believes that it is bad for business and for staff motivation. But it consis-

---

*Let me add a personal note: A close friend of mine operates in the world of music rather than business. Whenever I mention that I met someone or discussed an issue "over lunch," he bursts into laughter, saying this has happened so often that he believes all business is conducted over lunch—while I am left to ponder a growing paunch.

tently underrates the intelligence of its audience, who usually know more about the business than is envisaged. On the other hand, good-news propaganda is easy to identify. As a result, much of corporate communication only succeeds in breeding mistrust and cynicism.

Finally, managers are bad listeners. They have been taught that their role is to lead, but the concept has been interpreted to mean that seeking subordinates' views or listening to others is diminution of the leadership role or even an attack on their status. Perhaps the most important skill that needs to be encouraged in the national schools' curriculum, and most certainly in business schools, is the ability to *listen*.

Evasive Language

Technical jargon and business-speak cause confusion, but there is also the more dangerous variant of deliberately evasive language. An executive statement that "We are appraising our communications culture to bring our decision makers closer to our customers," which really means that the workforce is to be downsized by 40 percent, is bad enough. A company report like the Union Carbide example cited in Chapter 1 is an obscenity. A wilfully distorted message is also an insult to the intelligence of its recipients.

A recent study of company reports showed that using abstract, evasive language is a sure sign that the company is doing badly. Successful companies are those that have the confidence to send out clear messages. Plain English pays.

External Communication

In the preceding chapter, we discussed some of the issues involved in communicating with customers; in the next chapter we discuss communication with employees. But organizations do not exist or work in a vacuum. There are many outside organizations, groups, interests, and individuals who can influence or limit business performance. Here we should touch on considerations in communicating with outside parties, including:

suppliers
providers and owners
regulatory bodies
special-interest groups
community at large

Suppliers

Traditionally, communication with suppliers has been adversarial in nature. Purchasing departments or agents aim to buy at the lowest possible price, and all trust between the parties is gone, sacrificed on the altar of short-term profit. Now, however, more and more companies are recognizing that this approach to suppliers is counterproductive, though having said this, I'll mention that areas of the public sector that are being driven by so-called market factors have still had a tendency to follow the outdated traditional approach of lowest tender only.

Managers should try to reverse roles and consider their own position as a customer of their suppliers, to correctly anticipate the latter's own needs. It is just possible that the suppliers have the same problems in determining the needs of their own customers as do the managers.

Major corporations such as Marks and Spencer, Compaq, Hewlett-Packard, Wal-Mart, and J. Sainsbury establish long-term relationships with their suppliers on the basis that they share common interests and goals. These companies recognized years ago that pressurizing suppliers on price by using the weight of their buying power was against their best interests since awarding purchase contracts on price alone inevitably meant compromising quality. These corporations also realized that a host of problems involving suppliers are caused by the ordering company, usually through evasive or fuzzy communication.

Partnerships of interest cannot be established with a horde of competitive suppliers for each product. How would the buying company react toward its customers if orders were fragmented or switched arbitrarily to maintain price pressure? This approach ignores the cost of evaluating new suppliers and the time lost in changing from one supplier to another. Multisupply also introduces greater variation into work processes and thus mediates against the objective of *reducing* variation. Companies committed to continuous improvement are demanding the same from their suppliers. The first step on that path is to move toward single sourcing and then help the chosen supplier meet the buyer's objectives. This entails open communication based on the concept that the supplier wants to do a good job—indeed, the supplier wants to delight the customer.

Close collaboration with suppliers should be a planned two-way communication exercise. Selection obviously takes into account technical and financial competence, but it should also be extended to consider the personality and culture of the supplying company:

◉ Will it be able to share similar principles and values?
◉ How does it value its workforce?
◉ How well does it communicate, both internally and externally?
◉ Is it prepared to change with us?
◉ Is it likely to make a good long-term partner?

The answer to the last question is partly answered by the degree to which both parties have been able to reach an identity and established trust during communication. Successful communication with suppliers can make a major contribution to improved business performance.

Providers and Owners

Every organization is dependent on investment of financial resources into implementing its strategy and plans. In the commercial sector, these resources are provided by owners and shareholders. In the public sector, the resources ultimately come from the electorate. It would be unwise for an organization to omit these providers from its communications strategy.

Each type of provider has its own characteristics, which need to be taken into account in planning communication, but they all have one thing in common: They all want to know what the organization is doing with their money. Presentation of financial accounts, business performance, and forecasts is thus a major factor in communicating with providers. However, like all types of communication, these presentations must take into account the perception of the recipients.

Owners may be individuals, a family, or another company. They tend to have much closer contact with, and day-to-day interest in, the company than general shareholders do. In many cases, indeed, these providers initiate communication, usually in a questioning mode. As each situation is unique, there are no special points to make other than to say that all the rules of communication apply.

Shareholders

For purposes of planning communication, shareholders can be divided into institutional shareholders and private shareholders. It is also important to pay attention to the parties that influence investors, such as brokers, analysts, and the financial press.

Most public companies are effectively owned by a small number of institutions. According to Richard Hews of Ludgate Communications, there are a number of far-reaching trends currently at work that can affect institutional attitudes. Two are worth mentioning here: (1) Institutions are consolidating to form even larger organizations able to take bigger blocks of shares in companies and, as a result, to exercise greater influence over those companies; and (2) some large institutions are prepared to invest significantly in underperforming companies in order to stimulate, and if necessary enforce, change when this is seen to be desirable.

Private shareholders receive the reports and accounts of the company and are invited to the annual general meeting, and more regular contact can be designed to promote interest in the operations of their company. They are influenced by the financial press, advertising, targeted discounts, and special offers for the company's products or services. Shareholders can be invited to in-house company events and provided with a regular newsletter.

Informing the electorate can be a complicated issue. Many organizations promulgate a simple statement only to be caught in the crossfire from party political conflict. If the intention of the communication is to support a particular policy of one political party, make this clear without rancor or emotional argument.

Remember that next time it may involve a new policy and another party. In general, be aware of political nuances in dealing with the electorate, and keep to simple facts and examples.

Regulatory Bodies

Many of the current environmental regulations on pollution were resisted fiercely at their inception but are now accepted. This resistance is understandable as many of these regulations impose onerous costs of compliance on those being regulated. A small proportion of regulations, however, are downright stupid and reflect total ignorance of the situation. These are usually the result of mindless bureaucracy.

The vast majority of regulations are published in some form of draft before they become "law." Organizations should monitor these drafts so that they are in a position to communicate their viewpoint or take into account other opinions that could help in formulating the regulations in the most favorable context. Large corporations are likely to use permanent consultants and lobbyists to ensure that their positions are protected. Small companies should anticipate regulations in collaboration with representatives in their trade association, chamber of commerce, or other bodies, and then encourage these bodies to lobby on their behalf. This is another area to be included in the communications strategy to ensure that at the very least the issue is not neglected and that the resulting regulations do not come as a great surprise.

Special Interest Groups

There are a growing number of special interest groups competing for the attention of companies and the media. Many are worthy causes requesting support, or more specifically donations, irrespective of whether their cause has anything to do with the business. Others, however, can create undesirable publicity or steadily build perceptions up to crisis proportions.

Charitable donations are a straightforward issue of policy and can be viewed as a passive element of community relations. The policy issues are related to the amounts donated, the selection that brings the greatest benefit, and the degree of empowerment granted to the local operation to make its own decisions based on local knowledge and priorities. Only the board of the company can decide on thorny issues of, for example, political contributions.

An individual organization or company may become involved or targeted as part of a campaign by a special interest group without notice or reasonable expectation. This can involve company spokespersons in a conflict with the media for which they are ill equipped. During a major crisis, it quickly becomes apparent that events can be driven by the media. The task of management is to take control of the situation by being prepared and by anticipating the needs of the media.

The Community at Large

Active involvement in the community, as opposed to the easier passive option of sending a check, is becoming an important issue in the marketplace. With greater selectivity in employment, companies are conscious that any reputation they gain in the community helps them attract the best potential staff. Major retailers have taken the lead in proactive community involvement. The "Side by Side" initiative of J. Sainsbury is typical of the best in the field. This involves identifying a number of not-for-profit organizations and then getting groups of Sainsbury's staff to meet them and see what they can do and how they might help. Apart from the contribution to the community, Sainsbury believes that this initiative and its involvement programs enhance understanding, self-confidence, and development of young managers.

For a large corporation, successful involvement and communication with the community depends on overall policy guidance and resources from the center. This policy should be deployed to provide a universal message to all employees, seeking ownership of the need and responsive local management that will develop actions tailored to local conditions. Although most organizations are pleased to accept financial contributions, what they really value is recognition, friendship, and genuine involvement.

Keep Talking and Listening

In this chapter, we have seen that there are many ramifications to communication at work. We have stressed that business communication does not happen by accident, and that it is not a series of one-shot events. Communication is a process rather than a program.

The responsibility for developing a communications strategy and a corporate communications culture lies with senior management or leaders of the organization. To be successful, these developments often require fundamental change in management behavior. Senior management must constantly reinforce the focus on the communications strategy. None of this happens just because executives want it to happen. As we have seen, the practice of management and corporate history have helped create many barriers to communication. Specific actions and resources are required to dismantle these barriers and create a communications culture.

Questions for the Reader

1. Are you aware of a communications strategy in your organization?
2. How well does your organization communicate with the outside world?
3. Are you ever confused by mixed messages in company communication?
4. Who listens to you?

Chapter 12

People

Our experience proves that a policy of good human relations results in self-discipline, staff stability, good service to the customer, high productivity, and good profits in which we all share: employees, shareholders, pensioners, and the community.

Lord Sieff, former chairman, Marks and Spencer

It is the responsibility of the leadership and the management to give opportunities and put demands on people which enable them to grow as human beings in their work environment.

Sir John Harvey-Jones, former CEO of Imperial Chemical Industries

Well, we can't stand here doing nothing; people will think we're workmen.

Spike Milligan, British comedian

A whole new attitude to employment and development of people is required for tomorrow's business. Management must recognize that the more the demand rises for skilled people, the more those people will in turn demand a share in determining or at least influencing their own destiny. Evolutionary companies are already demonstrating that open communication, empowerment, and education and training of their people are decisive factors in their success. The corporation that forms a partnership with its people releases massive potential for the good of both the company and its customers. Toyota claims that its own people development and empowerment policies have created a companywide environment of teamwork that produces a million worthwhile suggestions from its workforce every year.

Again, there is no prescriptive answer in the shape of a tried and proven set of employment and recruitment policies. But for the organization that wants to improve relations with its people, this could start by reviewing and assessing every one of its recruitment, payment, communication, and development processes, policies, and procedures. The assessment criteria should be based on the degree to which each contributes to self-esteem, teamwork, innovation, competence, and desire to drive forward within the values of the company. A crucial element in establishing a working partnership of company and people is communication.

The Changing Workplace

The convergence of technologies, the growing proportion of knowledge workers, and the evolution of rising expectations are themselves converging to have a profound effect on the workplace. In particular, the traditional relationship between the employer and the employee is changing dramatically. There is considerable evidence of this change and its likely direction in sectors of the service industry and some specialized high-tech areas in manufacturing. However, like most evolutions it takes longer than expected for new patterns of employment to become general. There is still time to think and prepare for this new era in industrial relations.

The world of work is currently in the first stage of this evolution. Our evolutionary companies, as we noted in our discussion in Chapters 4 and 6 about self-directed teams and knowledge workers, are well past that stage and are developing their personnel policies and people for the later stages. Procter and Gamble, Hewlett-Packard, Canon, Sony, Toyota, and others are experimenting and putting into practice new employer-employee practices in collaboration with their employees. The traditional pyramid is disappearing, to be replaced with a bag of marbles—a collection of independent units continuously changing their personnel and relationships to tackle project after project. The corporate objective is to coordinate and communicate effectively with the "white spot" on the marbles, to create a cohesive whole. However, this takes time as the corporation moves through the intermediate stages of a flatter structure, thinking small, and finally releasing the potential of directed knowledge.

In contrast, the world's leading consultancies have promoted this restructuring as the latest cash cow. They have convinced many corporations to take revolutionary steps toward the new shape of industry based on technology. But there are too many other social and business interfaces to successfully make such a transition at this stage. James O'Shea and Charles Martin Madigan have devoted their book *Dangerous Company* to an examination of this phase. Perhaps the most pertinent story of misuse of consultants in this area is their researched description of the fiasco at Figgie International. Between 1989 and 1994, Figgie International spent more than $75 million in fees to some of America's most prestigious management consulting firms to move from a major player in the Fortune 500 to near bankruptcy. Sales of $1.3 billion in 1989 plunged to $319 million by 1994; profits of $63 million had turned into losses of $166 million. But they achieved the first objective; instead of seventeen thousand employees Figgie's workforce was indeed reduced—to about six thousand. Is it any wonder that demotivation and fear stalk the workplace whenever those survivors hear the words *change management*?

This evolution leads to contracted and subcontracted relationships with employees rather than loyal and committed employees of the corporation. We are already seeing a substantial increase in part-time rather than full-time jobs. Current thinking concentrates on the collapse of trust between employer and employee and the growing lack of security for a workforce that can no longer look forward to a job for life even if they perform adequately. The platonic Jeremiahs are forecasting doom and despondency for employer-employee relationships. Yet the reality can be exciting, different, and positive.

Evolutionary companies anticipate a very different future and are investing to achieve it through developing their personnel policies, education and training, and *participation* with their employees. Consider for a moment both sides of the coin in industrial relationships:

Positive View	*Negative View*
◉ Security and a job for life	◉ Wage slave, subject to the whims of autocratic managers
◉ Full-time work	◉ Locked into the corporate schedule
◉ Company loyalty	◉ Constrained individual freedom of action and thought

The challenge for evolutionary companies is to find a balance. This is particularly difficult during transition or evolution of the concepts. Their great strength in meeting this challenge is the high degree of trust and participation that has been engendered between employer and employee over the course of earlier evolutions. Together they are seeking a win-win solution to meeting the demands of the customer-focused global market. We have noted before that change often takes us back to where we once were. Conceptually, the move toward the independent-contractor knowledge worker is not unlike the relationship of the individual craftsman to the merchant prior to the industrial revolution.

From the point of view of talented and assiduous workers, this is the opportunity to define and control their destinies in line with their complete life aspirations: freedom to choose when they want to work and with whom; and freedom to manage their own time, so taking full account of social aspirations such as family and outside interests. The level of wealth for a large number of people is determined by their *own decisions* on the balance of choice between work and play.

From the point of view of the corporation (or perhaps more aptly described, the corporate coordinator), the coming era provides massive opportunities to provide a flexible response to every situation it faces in an evolving marketplace. The inertia of the corporate heavyweight can be replaced with the fast footwork and fast punching of the flyweight boxer.

In looking to the future, I am strongly positive in my attitude to changes in the workplace. I see a wonderful opportunity to release the energies and imagination of those involved. But I have retained an uncomfortable feeling about those who become excluded from the benefits of change. It is already possible to detect the growth of an underclass excluded from the aspirations of these evolutions. Perhaps that is the subject for another book; most certainly, in anticipating change it is a movement that must not be ignored. Successful business also requires a stable society.

Employee Focus

If we are to sustain the level of customer focus we discussed in Chapter 10, there needs to be a similar focus on employee communication. Evolutionary companies see employees as their internal customers, who also have needs and expectations. They recognize that employees have valuable knowledge of what is really happening in the organization.

Successful communication between management and employees can forge a partnership of interest in delighting the external customers. Yet too often management and employees act as adversaries, with the customers the victims of this war. Even enlightened management can fall into the trap of communicating *at* rather than *with* employees. It recognizes the need to keep employees in the picture, and it takes great trouble in formulating the message, varying the briefing media and encouraging feedback, but all still fails. Such employee communication systems are essentially one-way, as it is management that usually sets the agenda.

For successful communication at work, management must provide the means and the *permission* for employees to set some agendas of their own. Business needs open communication systems that allow speedy communication from workers about the problems that they are currently facing or are anticipating—problems that interfere with the objective of delighting customers. Organizations that ignore this facet soon find themselves on the rocks.

The best companies have always taken communication with their employees as a crucial element in the success of the organization. Others may need to establish a communications strategy to be effective.

Employee Communications Strategy

Developing and implementing an effective strategy for two-way employee communication organizationwide is dependent on the following elements:

- Creating and maintaining an environment or culture that supports employee communication
- Ensuring line-management comprehension, commitment, and skills to support the strategy
- Empowering and involving employees in implementing the strategy

As we look at each of these elements, we should be aware that the specific actions involved differ for each organization; the prevailing environments are unique, and actions should always match the particular culture.

The Culture

The environment or culture of the organization must be conducive to open and purposeful communication, or it does not thrive. The culture of an organization is assessed from the day-to-day actions and behavior of its members. These are governed by the *real* value systems, which are not necessarily those written down or expressed by its leaders. The environment is thus based on the *perceptions* that drive the actions of those involved, and these can be in direct conflict with stated values. Organizational culture is established by how management acts rather than by what it says.

A communications strategy should therefore start with some form of assessment of both the real organizational culture and barriers to successful communication. Assessment should help to decide whether to develop a communications strategy to change the culture, or whether to use the prevailing culture to support and improve communication with employees. The points to be covered in preparing a communications strategy can be summarized:

- Developing or reinforcing a culture where values come to mean more than just words on a mission statement
- Communicating company values to support the strategy and to ensure that the organization is open to change
- Ensuring that the strategy can cope with a vast amount of information and interfaces in times of change
- Achieving consistency in communication despite different cultural and language perceptions
- Using the strategy as an agent of change, and helping employees understand both what will change and what this change means for them

Every organization already contains a communications network established by the employees to fill the vacuum created by the lack of open management communication: the gossip network, which can be powerful and highly effective. Unfortunately, this is fed by rumor and false messages, and as such it can also be dangerous and destructive to employee morale and attitudes. The best way to counter the gossip network is to implement a communications network that empowers employees to give feedback and ensures that this feedback is demonstrably acted upon. In particular, the network should:

- Allow information, questions, comments, and opinions to travel through the organization
- Ensure that managers have the answers to questions, and that they indicate where and how information is available
- Build employee trust in the communications process so that honest feedback becomes a part of the natural way of working
- Remember that humor can break down many perceived barriers
- Overcome the barriers to communication associated with differing perceptions of the recipients in different divisions, locations, or parts of a unit
- Create an understanding both of different roles and of the need for collaboration in the organization by encouraging discussion and debate between employees in different functions and at different levels

Eliminating Conflicting Messages

Management is prone to send messages to external audiences, such as shareholders and customers, that are different from those sent to employees, and the meanings of these different messages are often in conflict. The role of management is to:

- Ensure that there is no conflict between the message that is given to employees and the one given to the external market
- Ensure that the internal communications operation and the public-relations department collaborate and give equal weight to internal and external communication
- Realize that bad internal messages and gossip eventually reach external recipients also
- Ensure that the employees' trust in internal channels of communication is not broken by their hearing messages *first* via external channels
- Ensure that the internal and external communication policies both stem from the same strategic considerations

Establishing Meaningful Measures

What you cannot measure, you cannot manage. This is as true for so-called soft projects as for other areas of business performance. The criteria for meaningful measurement both of the effectiveness of the communications strategy and of the benefits it brings to the business should be established from the outset and included in the plan. They should cover the following activities:

- Tracking the extent to which messages have reached all intended recipients
- Measuring (by interviews or questionnaire) the degree of understanding of the message, changing perceptions and attitudes of employees, and behavior and communications skills of managers
- Ensuring that the measures are realistic and focus on a few specific areas at a time

⊛ Relating the measurement trends and results to overall business performance

Management Behavior

A successful employee communications strategy ultimately depends upon the behavior of the line managers. Managers who listen to the views and interpretations of those involved are better placed to make the right implementation decisions. They are also likely to have a better understanding of employee attitudes and are thus better placed to remove barriers to communication.

An employee, whose opinion has been honestly sought and listened to is much more likely to respond positively to management messages. If the reasons for decisions are clearly explained, individuals most often respond enthusiastically, even if the decision runs counter to their opinion. They also have self-esteem because they have been recognized and treated with respect by their managers.

Training Managers in Communication Skills

Most line managers believe that training their people in communication skills is a worthwhile exercise. Unfortunately, they also believe that they are in their posts because they are good communicators, and that they themselves therefore don't need training in these skills. There is a tendency for managers to believe that their role is to make decisions and then communicate them to the employees. In their own mind, *communicate* is a synonym for *tell*. Successful communication at work is designed to ensure both better decisions and collaboration in implementing these decisions. It is not designed to remove responsibility for policy or decision making from management; indeed, it is the role of management to help people achieve work tasks. However, the very best managers also recognize that they need help from their people.

The most essential element in management development is to instill the belief in managers that they are now leading; this is a belief that provides inner confidence or self-esteem so that they are prepared to be vulnerable. It is also important to understand that disagreement from peers or subordinates, openly expressed, is not necessarily a sign of disrespect. Confident mangers realize that "soft" or caring management does not mean weak management. A manager who seeks others' views—even strong disagreement—before making and explaining a decision wins respect and intense loyalty from employees. That is leadership, not mere management.

Performance Measurement

Management keeps focused on the importance of communication if its performance measurements include measuring its level of competency in communication skills. Initial and appraisal interviews should ensure agreement on the communication competencies included in the specific job profile. Competency in employee communications should be an essential element in recognizing management performance. The concepts of "upward appraisal" and 360 degree feedback can be helpful in maintaining this focus.

Empowerment of Employees

Empowerment means giving employees the responsibility, authority, and resources to act on their own initiative in a growing arena of business operations. By definition, this should also change the way senior management traditionally communicates with employees. Empowerment also implies that employees have been given *permission* to communicate with management about the problems they are encountering in meeting their new responsibilities. Therefore, we are now considering two-way communication about an employee-determined agenda.

Earlier, we noted the barrier of language in achieving real two-way communication. The key to solving this problem is to establish the common language of measurement as a tool to control work and workers. In the changed circumstances of the information age, the most effective step that management can take in empowering employees is to allow them to measure rather than be measured.

Continuous measurement—and *display of the measures*—of the work processes in which employees engage can change the whole culture of an organization. All the previously hidden frustrations and hassles related to work are now open for discussion in an objective environment. There is nothing esoteric in this simple solution to many of the problems in business. All it needs is commitment to thorough education and training of both management and employees in the concept and practice of appropriate measurement in their business operations. Measurement is not only an important element in two-way communication; it is also the outward sign of inward grace for the successful organization.

Teamwork

Teamwork is the basis for a whole new way of working toward delighting customers and gaining competitive advantage. Teamwork can be simply defined as management and employees working together to continuously improve their business processes. Successful communication of company values is the glue that unites teams in a single purpose.

Recognition

A confident and proud workforce adds colossal value to the overall performance of an organization. An employee who enjoys confidence and self-esteem as part of a team feels pride in both his or her work and the company. Management recognition of the worth of employees as individuals is a determining factor in developing this attitude among employees.

Research has proved that recognition in its many forms is more important than rewards, including money incentives. A sense of worth gives meaning to the life and work of the individual. There are many different types of recognition, and these must be selected to suit the individual and the circumstances. They encompass praise, more responsibility and authority, professional recognition, and a sense of accomplishment in the work situation. Recognition is reinforced when it is then communicated to peers and others involved with the individual.

When recognizing individuals for their contribution in the workplace, it is also important to recognize their worth to others in their outside environment. Recognition that involves family, friends, and others in the individual's community is doubly effective in establishing self-esteem and confidence.

Tomorrow's Managers

We are watching an evolution in management styles that to some extent is a difference in generations. Older managers find it difficult to move easily from the macho-boss style of their own development to the style of the team leader, who has to win the respect of all their people. They also face very different circumstances in the workplace.

In tomorrow's workplace, workers will not be dutifully waiting for instructions or neatly concentrated in departments. They are more likely to be spread across the country—or in another country altogether. Control cannot therefore be exercised through meetings and memos. Indeed, the whole concept of the control of people will be outdated as employees become self-determined users of knowledge. The manager, or team leader, will seek to control processes, not people, through coordination of resources and requirements.

This evolution requires a different emphasis on attributes in developing future managers. These attributes include team working, high interpersonal skills, negotiating, consensus management, and the ability to handle several issues or projects at a time. It is interesting that these are the attributes that social evolution has developed in women. Female ways of managing life are much better suited to tomorrow's business than is traditional male behavior.

The new leaders face a number of challenges in the flatter and more dispersed organization of tomorrow. They are coordinating multidisciplinary teams and aiming to maximize the brainpower potential of all employees. This depends on developing competence and trust in the employees to make their own decisions. Knowledge is the key, so the organization must commit itself to a high level of investment in people and management development. The old career-path ladder is disappearing. Employee satisfaction comes from continuously extending the interest and diversity of their roles. In this environment, people take control of their destiny by committing to themselves to lifelong learning.

Education and Training

Evolutionary companies have already recognized that the most powerful vehicle available to them to build a partnership with their people is education and training. There is a difference. In business, we want to influence employee attitudes so that they take common ownership of the values of the organization. Education also plays a part in giving employees the confidence to think for themselves within the horizons of those values. Training is directed toward competence in the corporation's field and in developing the techniques of management. In this context, managing change is a core competency.

Adult learning in business is most effective when it directly relates to the workplace. Employees at all levels are more likely to understand and retain knowledge if they have an easy transition with practice of the new concepts in their own work (Figure 12-1).

In such an environment, in-house instructors are more effective than external specialists. Preferably, the in-house instructors are also fellow managers or knowledge workers rather than professional trainers from the education department. To some extent, this is governed by the subject and the existing level of

Figure 12-1. Principles of adult education.

THEORY → PRACTICE → ACTION

knowledge within the organization. But it does indicate that an important element in management development should be teaching mechanics. We noted earlier that managers need to spend their working lives acquiring knowledge; a sensible additional value would be that they must always commit to *sharing* knowledge.

Unfortunately, though executives readily accept the theory of this educational concept, they rarely put it fully into practice and their resulting actions can be counterproductive. They have a growing tendency to accept the need for substantial investment in education and training and then organize budgets to provide the resource. Having played their part as responsible leaders (in their view), they now delegate implementation of the educational strategy to the specialist HR and training departments.

The purpose of the educational element is to ensure ownership of the organization's purpose and values. The responsibility to develop and communicate the purpose and values is an executive role. The purpose of the training element is to provide competence in all the operational areas of the company. The responsibility to deploy relevant competencies lies with operational management. In other words, the CEO and senior operational management must play comprehensive roles in developing the material content of all education and training. It cannot be easily delegated.

Education and training is the primary strategic vehicle for success in a knowledge-based global competitive world. It is *the* priority for the CEO and his or her immediate colleagues. "Our people are our major asset," we hear. The real message is, "Walk the talk!"

Questions for the Reader

1. Does your own organization have a clearly defined development program for everyone?
2. Regarding your own commitment to your own development, what actions are in your schedule?
3. Attempt to list what you need or desire for your own potential to be realized. Try to allocate the items between education and training.

4. Do you play any part in the education and training of your colleagues?
5. How much is your opinion sought?
6. Define the most positive element in the company's communication.
7. Are there any weaknesses in the company's communication?
8. What could you do to improve communication?

Chapter 13

Stewardship

The way to success in business is honesty and fair dealing. If you can fake that, you've got it made.

Groucho Marx

Your legacy should be that you made it better than it was when you got it.

Lee Iacocca, former CEO, Chrysler Corporation

A leader is one who sees the whole situation, organizes the experience of the group, offers a vision of the future, and trains followers to be leaders.

Mary Parker Follett

Stewardship

Several of our evolutionary companies started out as small family businesses, and some have remained fundamentally under family ownership. This is not surprising, as one thing that all the evolutionary companies seem to share is most recognizable in the family-owned business: the critical value of stewardship. To my knowledge, only Arthur Andersen spells it out as one of their specific values, but all the others appear to exhibit it as an element in their consistent success.

Webster's dictionary defines *stewardship* as "moral responsibility for the careful use of money, time, talents, or other resources—especially with respect to the principles or needs of a community or group." In a period of change, this would appear to be a very powerful value and reference point for any organization or institution intending to survive the vicissitudes of history and change. Evolution could be seen as a continuous state of change. This is unsettling to many organizations, which build in an inertia that acts as a barrier to commonsense development, but change without some constant reference point is not a comfortable human situation. The organization would be cast adrift on a vast sea without a compass.

This approach to change with stewardship as the constant reference point is illustrated in Figure 13-1. Leaders of corporations, just like families, inherit an organization and its essential values. It is the role of the leader to hand over an improved organization with the core values intact. It has long been the practice of Arthur Andersen for the lead partner at periodic stages to present a paper to the assembled partners on their *collective stewardship* of the firm.

The day-to-day operations of the organization are beset with a series of situations in which people have to decide how to surmount the natural barriers of resistance and general inertia. But every now and then, one of these situations poses a danger to the organization in what at first sight looks like an opportunity. These are the dangers of mindless change or revolution. An individual evangelist leader, or a common external mood, can sometimes so infect an organization that the change is worshiped in its own right. Then during implementation the change gets un-

Figure 13-1. Stewardship.

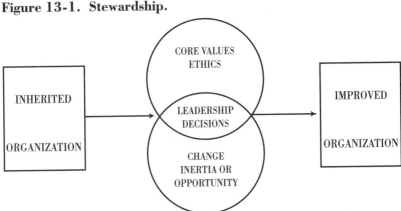

bridled and out of control, to the ultimate extent that it can lead to destruction of the organization.

A leadership that has grown to absorb the real meaning of the company's values and ethics will use them at all times as a reference point for decisions. This is why so many of the evolutionary companies recruit their leaders from within; they do not want to risk accepting leaders from outside even if they're ostensibly brilliant. That in reality is the practice of stewardship.

Responsibility

Corporations have a social and ethical responsibility that is wider than collaborative community activity and charitable contributions. Many corporate leaders fear that global competition between businesses, with its need to drive down costs and seek new markets, will defeat considerations of good corporate citizenship. Business has moved on from the days when companies carried on irresponsible environmental policies until a disaster or some element of the media caught them out. Now there is much more commitment to preventive and proactive conduct. Since Chernobyl and Bhopal, most organizations have come to realize that the most efficient way to deal with an environmental problem is to avoid creating it. Increasingly, there is recognition that good environmental performance means good business performance.

Of course, there are also external pressures on business to help them come to that recognition. There are a growing number of adequately funded regulatory bodies to inspect and penalize the nonperformers. Business lobbyists do continually complain that all these activities surrounding environmental standards are expensive and impose noncompetitive costs on companies. Well, of course—but that's the purpose, to ensure that the perpetrators pay the costs up front rather than have much greater costs inflicted on the community as a whole. The other principal pressure comes from pressure groups and their natural allies in the media. Several great corporations such as Texaco, Exxon, and McDonald's have paid a substantial price in customer loyalty as a result of the power of the "green" lobby.

There is a tendency to view environmental responsibility as

only a concern for governments and large corporations. The Boston Park Plaza Hotel, the largest family-run hotel in the United States, has turned its hotel into an environmental showcase and demonstrated that dramatic results can be achieved by relatively small companies. In 1990, the hotel completely revamped its policies and procedures to incorporate a business philosophy "that weighs the environmental impact of everything we do while maintaining our high standards of guest service and quality."* Their "Environmental Action Program" is designed to conserve energy and water, reduce waste and eliminate hazardous waste, and generally concentrate on recycling. Tedd Saunders, a member of the owning family, is the environmental program director; he states that the program is "not only to impact our daily operations, but also to reflect our long-term commitment to the earth." This program has achieved such fame that Saunders has published a book on the subject, entitled *Green Is Black*, and set up a separate consultancy to assist other organizations.

Just to list a few of these results is to indicate what a dramatic impact on the environment could be achieved if this concern for the environment became a widely accepted corporate value:

- Eliminated polystyrene foam, plastic tableware, and aerosols throughout the hotel
- Created bathroom amenities systems that are eliminating use of two million plastic containers annually
- Initiated recycling programs for paper, steel, printer cartridges, cardboard, shipping pallets, aluminum, glass, plastic, telephone books, and newspapers
- Installed 1,686 double-glazed windows, faucet aeration, and water-efficient shower heads in all 977 guest rooms

These and other small actions have added up to big savings. Each year this program saves:

16.5 million gallons of water
300 trees (via paper recycling)

*Tedd Saunders, *Green Is Black* (New York: HarperCollins, 1993).

300,000 pieces of plastic dishware
29,000 gallons of fuel oil
200,000 pounds of "trash" (242 dumpster loads)

That is taking stewardship to a much wider plane than that of business performance.

Ethics

At one time, *business ethics* rivaled *military intelligence* as the most popular example of the oxymoron. Steadily, as the concept of corporate responsibility has grown, there has been a change of perception of the importance of business ethics. There is still considerable confusion about what part it plays in the corporation and in particular how to teach the subject. However, it is generally recognized as an important issue for corporate leadership. To paraphrase Aristotle, "It is hard to be ethical; otherwise we would not praise it."

The rise of business ethics as a specific subject for universities, business colleges, and the corporation developed in the United States in the 1960s. It started as a reaction to a series of bribery scandals involving American corporations in the United States and overseas and the rise of the New Frontier issues of civil rights, women's liberation, and the environment. Public pressure on health and environmental safety, and to an extent moral consciousness of exploitation of the third world, have accelerated interest in how business should be conducted ethically within free-market conditions.

Corporate executives and managers are still confused about their role in ethics. Many understand it as some form of code of conduct that prohibits employees from accepting or giving bribes, dumping chemical waste in rivers, or cheating on their expense forms. Slowly, a realization is at last emerging that ethics is an issue of corporate responsibility rather than a matter of how individual executives and managers perform.

We have noted the problems that have arisen with the disappearance of the foundation element of business education. There is a similar issue in the teaching of ethics. Some business schools feel that ethics cannot be taught without a grounding in philosophy, so that students are enabled to take ownership of the concept. Others feel strongly that this is old-fashioned lecturing and what students really need is case-history teaching that provides them with concrete answers to the ethical problems they will face in real business. It is extremely doubtful that a concrete set of commandments from a case history guided Johnson and Johnson to their ethical action on the Tylenol scare; it was a natural consequence of the ethical foundation enshrined in their credo or value systems. Nevertheless, Johnson and Johnson's action provided a powerful boost to the whole concept of business ethics, not least because in the long run it was demonstrated to be good business. They have formed a bond of trust with their customers that no amount of advertising or promotion could ever buy.

Though the real ownership of business ethics is still evolving within corporate life, it is very clear that the whole debate has opened the door wider—or enlarged the perspective of corporations just by raising the moral issue as a discussion point in the boardroom. Business is also beginning to comprehend that as they become global, public opinion or customers are less tolerant of any abuse of internationally accepted codes of conduct.

Executives and even politicians who have not taken ownership of philosophical concepts of ethics tend to view even glaring abuses as related to individual misdeeds and having little to do with corporate management. There are aspects of that misconception in the recent Baring's Bank scandal in London and Singapore and the long-running issue of Swiss bankers' relationships with the German confiscation of property during the massacre of the Jews. As Lynn Sharp Paine pointed out in the *Harvard Business Review* of March 1994, "In fact, ethics has *everything* to do with management . . . unethical business practice involves the tacit, if not explicit, cooperation of others and reflects the values, attitudes, beliefs, language, and behavioral patterns that define an organization's operating culture."

Ethics, then, is an organizational issue and the corporation has the responsibility to see that its managers accept their role in establishing an ethical culture. They must institute systems and education and training that strengthen the relationships and reputations on which their company's success depends. They must exhibit leadership.

Leadership

A leading contributor to the debate about business ethics in the United States is Prof. Al Gini of Loyola University of Chicago. In exploring the intersection of business ethics and leadership in his paper to the Kellogg Leadership Studies Project (Kellogg Foundation, 1996), he emphasizes the role that "the witness of moral leadership" plays in improving the standards of business and organizational life. He echoes a theme of the present book in demonstrating that the fundamental principle is age-old and noting that Aristotle suggested that morality cannot be learned simply by reading a treatise on virtue. The spirit of morality, said Aristotle, is awakened through the virtues and conduct of a moral person. The "witness of another," or what we now refer to as a role model or mentor, is another fundamental principle. Gini is convinced that without "the continuous commitment, enforcement, and modeling of leadership, standards of business ethics cannot and will not be achieved in any organization." Leaders help set the tone, develop the vision, and shape the behavior of all those involved in both business and social life. The ethics of leadership affect the ethos of the workplace and thereby help to form the ethical choices and decisions of people in the workplace.

Leadership is hard to define, and moral leadership is even harder. We are unlikely to better that great management leader, Mary Parker Follett, in her description of a leader at the head of the chapter: "A leader is one who sees the whole situation . . . and trains followers to be leaders." Perhaps we can take shelter in the argument of American historian Garry Wills's assertion that "successful leaders need to understand their followers far more than followers need to understand leaders."

Trust

Stewardship, leadership, business ethics, and the art of management are perennial subjects of interest to those involved in business, or even to mere observers. The very best aspects of all these areas can be summed up in the word *trust*. The British business "guru" Charles Handy believes that trust will be critical in the workplace of tomorrow. He argues that what he calls "virtual organizations" are built on trust—which should be good news to management because it is cheaper to trust people than to regulate, inspect, and control them. But he raises a powerful question, the answer to which shapes the organization of tomorrow: "How can you trust someone you do not know?" As he points out, you cannot trust someone who is not committed to the goals and values of the organization, and you cannot trust people who let you down. As corporations wrestle with that question, they review their whole approach to recruitment and induction through probationary contracts. But Handy then asks, "How many people can you know well enough to trust?" Answers vary, but probably not more than fifty people. Thus the answer to successful empowerment through trust also defines the size of organizational units, which must get smaller and smaller and more stable so that people can get to know each other over time and create a bond of trust. What Handy's arguments make clear is that values like trust are not simple statements to be framed and hung in the foyer; they profoundly affect our working lives.

For the Reader

You may have read or browsed through this book from any of a number of perspectives. You will have noted that it is critical of the way that many managers of business have behaved in the past and are behaving now. From time to time, the book has also noted some attributes of the managers of successful evolutionary corporations that are intended as pointers for the future. The book has also argued that there has been an evolutionary change in management style, which is continuing. If you are a manager or an aspiring manager, or just an interested observer, consider from the list below which are your *predominant* characteristics:

Traditional Manager	*Evolutionary Manager*
⊙ Considers himself or herself as the manager or boss	⊙ Considers himself or herself as a team leader, mentor, and role model

Traditional Manager	*Evolutionary Manager*
⦿ Follows the defined chain of command	⦿ Deals with anyone necessary to make a decision or do the job
⦿ Has the confidence to make decisions alone	⦿ Accepts the responsibility but involves others in the decision
⦿ Manages information	⦿ Shares information
⦿ Concentrates on what he or she is best at, such as finance or marketing	⦿ Tries to master a number of management disciplines; forever learning
⦿ Always provides clear instructions for others	⦿ Trusts others
⦿ Accepts corporate rules and goals as the way the job is to be done	⦿ Constantly searches for a better way
⦿ Demands hard work; expects long hours as evidence of commitment	⦿ Demands results

Further Reading and References

Thousands of books have been published on the subject of management. The following selection includes books that have been referenced in the text and others that the author has found helpful. The list has been organized alphabetically by author.

Albrecht, Karl, *The Northbound Train* (New York: AMACOM, 1994).

Amis, Kingsley, *The King's English* (New York: HarperCollins, 1997).

Block, Peter, *Stewardship* (San Francisco: Berrett-Koehler, 1993).

Carr, Clay, *Choice, Chance, and Organizational Change* (New York: AMACOM, 1996).

Cemach, Harry P., and Lawe, F. W., *Work Study in the Office* (London: Office Magazine Ltd., 1958).

Collins, James C., and Porras, Jerry I., *Built to Last* (New York: HarperCollins, 1994).

Crainer, Stuart, *Leaders on Leadership* (London: Institute of Management Foundation, 1996).

Davies, Norman, *Europe: A History* (Oxford, England: Oxford University Press, 1996).

Dionne, E. J., *Why Americans Hate Politics* (New York: Simon & Schuster, 1992).

Eccles, Robert G., and Nohna, Nitin, *Beyond the Hype* (New York: McGraw-Hill, 1992).

Fisher, Kimball, and Fisher, Mareen D., *The Distributed Mind* (New York: AMACOM, 1997).

Fitz-Enz, Jac, *The 8 Practices of Exceptional Companies* (New York: AMACOM, 1997).

Follett, Mary Parker, *Prophet of Management* (Cambridge, Mass.: Harvard Business School Press, 1994).

Foster, Richard, *Innovation* (London: Guild, 1986).

Fritz, Robert, *The Path of Least Resistance* (New York: Fawcett, 1984).

Fukuyana, Francois, *Trust* (New York: Free Press, 1985).

Galbraith, John Kenneth, *The Anatomy of Power* (Boston: Houghton Mifflin, 1983).

―――― *The World Economy Since the Wars* (Boston: Houghton Mifflin, 1994).

Halberston, David, *The Fifties* (New York: Random House, 1993).

Hammer, Michael, and Champy, James, *Reengineering The Corporation* (New York: HarperCollins, 1993).

Handy, Charles, *Gods of Management* (London, Souvenier Press, 1978).

―――― *Understanding Organizations* (Oxford, England: Oxford University Press, 1992).

―――― *Age of Unreason* (Cambridge, Mass.: Harvard Business Press, 1989).

―――― *The Empty Raincoat* (New York: Random House, 1996).

Harrington, H. James, *The Improvement Process* (New York: McGraw-Hill, 1987).

Harrington-Mackin, Deborah, *The Team Building Tool Kit* (New York: AMACOM, 1997).

Harvey-Jones, John, *Making It Happen* (London: Guild, 1988).

Heller, Robert, *Modern Management* (London: Harrap, 1988).

―――― *The Naked Manager for the Nineties* (New York: Warner Press, 1995).

Kanter, Rosabeth Moss, *The Change Masters* (New York: Simon & Schuster, 1983).

―――― *When Giants Learn to Dance* (New York: Simon & Schuster, 1989).

Kennedy, Paul, *The Rise and Fall of the Great Powers* (New York: Random House, 1987).

Kinsman, Francis, *Millennium* (London: W. H. Allen, 1990).

Koontz, Harold, and O'Donnell, Cyril, *Principles of Management* (New York: McGraw-Hill, 1993).

Kotter, John P., *Leading Change* (Cambridge, Mass.: Harvard Business School Press, 1996).

Macdonald, John, *But We Are Different* (Management Books 2000, 1994).

Mahesh, V. S., *Thresholds of Motivation* (New York: McGraw-Hill, 1993).

McCormack, Mark H., *What They Don't Teach You at Harvard Business School* (New York: Bantam Books, 1986).

McRae, Hamish, *The World in 2020* (New York: HarperCollins, 1994).

Murphy, Kevin J., *Effective Listening* (New York: Bantam Books, 1987).

Naisbitt, John, *Global Paradox* (New York: William Morrow, 1994).

O'Shea, James, and Charles Martin Madigan, *Dangerous Company* (New York: Random House, 1997).

Parker Pen Company, *Do's and Don'ts: Taboos Around the World* (Janesville, Wis.: Parker Pen, 1985).

Pascale, Richard Tanner, and Athos, Anthony G., *The Art of Japanese Management* (New York: Simon & Schuster, 1981).

Ralston, Faith, *Hidden Dynamics* (New York: AMACOM, 1995).

Ranganathanada, Swami, *Eternal Values for a Changing Society* (Bombay: Bharam, 1958).

Saunders, Tedd, *Green Is Black* (New York: HarperCollins, 1993).

Senge, Peter, *The Fifth Discipline* (New York: Doubleday, 1994).

Sherriton, Jacalyn, and Stern, James L., *Corporate Culture, Team Culture* (New York: AMACOM, 1996).

Sieff, Marcus, *Don't Ask the Price* (London: George Weidenfeld and Nicholson Ltd., 1986).

Sorell, Tom, and Hendry, John, *Business Ethics* (Woburn, Mass.: Butterworth-Heinemann, 1994).

Tannen, Deborah, *You Just Don't Understand* (New York: Ballantine, 1990).

Tobin, Daniel R., *The Knowledge Enabled Organization* (New York: AMACOM, 1997).

Toffler, Alvin, *The Third Wave* (New York: Bantam Books, 1970).

——— *Future Shock* (New York: Bantam Books, 1970).

Tse, K. K., *Marks and Spencer* (New York: Pergamon Press, 1985).

Voght, Judith F., and Murrell, Kenneth L., *Empowerment in Organizations* (San Diego: Pfeiffer, 1990).

Wright, Peter, *Managerial Leadership* (New York: Routledge, 1996).

Wyden, Peter, *The Unknown Iacocca* (London: Sidgwick and Jackson Ltd., 1987).

Index